Bible
Pinnacles

BOOKS BY IVOR POWELL

BIBLE CAMEOS

These eighty graphic "thumb-nail" sketches are brief biographies of Bible people. Pungent and thought-provoking studies.

BIBLE HIGHWAYS

In this series of Bible studies, Scripture texts are linked together, suggesting highways through the Bible from Genesis to Revelation.

BIBLE PINNACLES

A spiritual adventure into the lives and miracles of Bible characters and the meaningful parables of our Lord.

BIBLE TREASURES

In refreshingly different style and presentation, these eighty Bible miracles and parables are vividly portrayed.

BIBLE WINDOWS

Anecdotes and stories are, in fact, windows through which the Gospel light shines, to illumine lessons for teachers and preachers.

MARK'S SUPERB GOSPEL

This most systematic study offers expositional, devotional and homiletical thoughts. The enrichment gained from the alliteration outlines will create a desire for more truth.

LUKE'S THRILLING GOSPEL

In this practical and perceptive commentary, there is a gold-mine of expository notes and homilies.

JOHN'S WONDERFUL GOSPEL

Another verse-by-verse distinctively different commentary with sermonic notes and outlines.

WHAT IN THE WORLD WILL HAPPEN NEXT?

An unusual work on prophecy dealing especially with the return of Christ to earth and the nation of Israel's future.

Bible
Pinnacles

by

Ivor Powell

Foreword by

F.W. Boreham

KREGEL PUBLICATIONS
Grand Rapids, Michigan 49501

Bible Pinnacles by Ivor Powell. Copyright © 1952 by Ivor Powell. Published 1985 by Kregel Publications, a division of Kregel, Inc. All rights reserved.

Library of Congress Cataloging in Publication Data

Powell, Ivor, 1910-
  Bible Pinnacles.

  Reprint. Originally published: London : Marshall, Morgan & Scott, 1952.
  Includes index.
  1. Bible—Biography. I. Title.
BS571.5.P66 1985   220.9'2   84-26136
ISBN 0-8254-3516-1
Printed in the United States of America

CONTENTS

FOREWORD

For some inscrutable reason, the Author has invited me to append to his illuminating volume an entirely superfluous Foreword. My affectionate admiration of Mr. Powell, and my deep appreciation of his fine work as an attractive writer and a victorious evangelist, render it a real pleasure to comply with his surprising request.

With wistful hearts, many of us envy the preacher who, possessing the personal equipment of an evangelist, and skilled in the delicate craftsmanship of wooing his fellow-men, is also endowed from on high with the divine power that will enable him to exercise triumphantly these superb gifts. To excel in this difficult department of the Christian ministry, a man needs the spirit of an evangelist; the message of an evangelist; and the technique of an evangelist. Many of us possess one or two of these qualifications; but happy indeed is the man who rejoices in all three!

Ivor Powell has much to teach us, and, in his " Bible Cameos " and " Bible Pinnacles," he pours his rich treasure amassed in the course of his world-wide experience into the hungry hearts of his eager readers. No man can sit at his feet without acquiring fresh skill in the sublime art of coaxing his fellow-men into the Kingdom of God.

Mr. Powell stands at the pulsing heart of the spiritual universe. He glorifies the Cross. Of its divine magnetism and resistless might he has no shadow of doubt. He is convinced that the paramount need of our tortured world is the need of a Saviour; and, as his earlier books conclusively prove, he wields a phenomenal—almost an uncanny—skill in capturing for Christ the hearts of the most unlikely and unpromising people.

The book is adorned by a fascinating title. Bible Pinnacles! The picturesque phrase presents to the imagination those snow capped and sky-piercing peaks that, on every continent, wrap their clouds about them and stand defiant and yet challenging. Much that Mr. Powell has to say is as bracing as those stinging breezes that hurl the hail into the flushed faces of the daring mountaineers who essay the steep ascent.

In all that he writes, Mr. Powell leads us up those beckoning slopes to the untrodden altitudes from which we catch breath-taking visions of boundless immensity, visions that could never have been ours had we remained among the foothills and the lowlands.

I breathe on "Bible Pinnacles" a most fervent benediction.

F. W. BOREHAM

PREFACE

Of all the books which have thrilled my soul during the years of my Christian ministry, the works of Dr. F. W. Boreham stand supreme. His choice language and superb illustrations are the products of a master artist, and oftentimes a page of his book has transported me to realms as enchanting as fairyland.

I remember a night when amidst desolate and very drab surroundings, I sat reading his description of Hobart in Tasmania. Dr. Boreham was at one time the minister of the Hobart Baptist Church, and in his own inimitable way he had described the impregnable grandeur of Hobart's Mount Wellington. As I read, I forgot my immediate surroundings and instantly stood with God's servant on the wonderful hill which overlooks the approaches to Tasmania's finest harbour. Little did I realize then that my dreams would come true; that my imagination would give place to reality.

In the early months of 1952, I became the guest of the Tasmanian Baptist Union, and during my visit to the picturesque island, I planned a visit to Hobart. I confess that I was drawn there by Dr. Boreham's living picture of Mount Wellington. Slowly I drove my car to the summit, and later, as I admired the panorama views, I relived the moments when first I had pictured the scene.

At that time also, this book was being written, and the magnificent splendour of the mountain peak seemed to suggest the Scriptures I was then trying to expound. The wonderful chapters of the Bible appeared as lofty viewpoints from which one could see all the country of the grace of God, and then, quite suddenly, " Bible Pinnacles " suggested itself as the ideal title for the new book. " Bible Cameos " and " Bible Pinnacles " are twin sisters, and both are sent forth with the earnest prayer that they might afford great assistance to all who preach or teach the Word of Life.

Dr. Boreham has graciously written the Foreword for this book, and it is not easy to express my appreciation of his contribution. He wistfully confessed to me on one occasion that he would have loved to be an evangelist. And yet when I listened to his preaching in the lunch hour meetings in the Scots' Church, Melbourne, I sighed and wished I could be as great an evangelist as Dr. Boreham. To him and to my publishers I express my sincere thanks, and trust this new book will bring joy to all its readers.

Australia   IVOR POWELL

BIBLE PINNACLES

EVE . . . God's first gift to man

(GENESIS 2:21-22)

> In a garden was laid a most beautiful maid
>   As ever was seen in the morn:
> She was made a wife the first day of her life,
>   And she died before she was born.

In these strange lines, someone has written the life story of the first woman—the first sweetheart—" the mother of all living." In every age God has undertaken for the need of His servants, but not the least among His great gifts was woman. Man would be unspeakably lonely if he were left to walk alone. Thus the Creator planned His first present for man, and in due course Adam was joined by Eve.

God's Great Power

Stillness reigned in the garden, for man had been put to sleep. The great Surgeon was about to perform His first operation, and all creation waited expectantly. The stately trees provided the shade for the hospital theatre, and the Holy Spirit arranged every detail according to the divine requirements. Man, buoyant, radiant, unsuspecting, was given earth's first anæsthetic; and as waves of increasing weariness swept over his tired eyes, he sank into the shadows, and the Surgeon smiled! Perhaps even the birds hushed their songs lest, inadvertently, they should waken the sleeper and so hinder the great work. Heaven's great Surgeon had been entrusted with the task, and with skill born of deity, He leaned over His patient. Gently, so gently, He closed the wounds, and looked at the unconscious patient. What a glad surprise would await Adam when he opened his eyes again! " And the rib, which the Lord had taken from man, made he a woman."

God's Great Pleasure

She was lovely; she was indescribably charming; as dignified as befitted the queen of creation; as refreshing as the morning dew. Her eyes were lit with enquiry and pleasure as she scanned her surroundings. Her movements were graceful and effortless, and when she spoke, pleasure thrilled the Creator's heart. She was fascinatingly beautiful; she was good, and very desirable. " And the Lord God brought her to man." Poor Adam, he was

1

dumbfounded! He wondered if this were a dream; if this goddess would disappear immediately he awakened. Then he rubbed his eyes. She was still there, and her friendly smiles added charm to her attractiveness. Poor man, he was shy; he was an inexperienced boy; he had never had a sweetheart. And then love was born in his soul. The wedding took place within the sacred precincts of God's open-air cathedral. God, the Father of the bride, gave her away; man's best Friend, the royal Surgeon, stood at the groom's side; and the Holy Spirit was the officiating minister. And when the service ended, the choirs of heaven sang their anthems. The honeymoon was spent within the restful tranquillity of God's holiday home, and as the two lovers walked hand in hand, all creation acclaimed the wisdom of the Lord.

God's Great Purpose.

They built their little home, and regularly the great Surgeon went down to visit them. They talked together, and planned for the future. Time passed by, until stark tragedy overwhelmed them. They sinned, and forfeited their joyous companionship with God. They were cast out of their garden home. But then, in their hour of shame and sorrow, a new miracle was performed, and the future grew bright again with promise. Eve shared her secret, and Adam's heart overflowed. He watched her quiet preparations, and when she smiled into his eyes, heaven filled his heart. They could hardly wait for the coming of their treasure; but ultimately the dream came true, and Eve looked into the starry eyes of her child. Perhaps her voice faltered when she said, " I have gotten a man from the Lord," and that night there were three at the family altar. And thus the purposes of God began to unfold. There, too, were the earliest foreshadowings of God's greatest miracle. He sees the end from the beginning, and away in the dim and distant ages He saw the day when the Last Adam, the great Surgeon Himself, would sink into a deep sleep. He saw the miracle that would be performed when, through the death of the cross, the bride of Christ would be brought into being. The Church, radiant as the morning, without spot or wrinkle, without blemish or sin, would be presented to the Bridegroom, and at the marriage supper of the Lamb highest heaven would ring with the songs of the redeemed.

CAIN AND ABEL . . . the first murder

(GENESIS 4:1-10)

Alas, tragedy had overtaken the happy couple, and their sorrow was all the more poignant because they realized they had lost their greatest opportunity. The Creator had desired to share with them eternal life, but everything had depended upon their choice. The tree of life had been placed in the midst of the garden, and had they taken of its fruit they would have partaken of the divine nature. Beguiled by the evil one, they had eaten at the wrong tree; and with the entrance of sin, the way to the tree of life had been closed. "Lest," said God, "they eat, and live for ever." They had lost their great opportunity, they had lost their sinlessness, they had lost their radiant joys; but—and this was their solitary comfort—they had not lost God. His grace had provided the coat of skins, and their shameful nakedness had been hidden.

The Simple Training.

The entrance of sin had corrupted their souls, and even if every subsequent action had been in accord with the will of God, their nature would yet have remained sinful. It became clear that evil had tainted their lives, and had been transmitted to their children. The understanding eyes of that first mother recognized the traits in the characters of her sons, and probably she ably supported her husband as he endeavoured to instruct his children. It has been said that Adam's home was the first Christian home in the world. Every day he taught his sons the lessons of life, and their religious instruction was not overlooked. He taught the truth which he himself had received from God. The sacrificial lamb had atoned for human guilt; the way to the divine heart was through an offering. Thus the two boys grew up in the atmosphere of a Sabbath school; but their knowledge brought added responsibility.

The Serious Trouble.

"Abel was a keeper of sheep, but Cain was a tiller of the ground. And . . . it came to pass, that Cain brought of the fruit of the ground an offering unto the Lord. And Abel, he also brought of the firstlings of his flock and of

3

the fat thereof. And the Lord had respect unto Abel and his offering: but unto Cain and to his offering he had not respect. And Cain was very wroth, and his countenance fell." Then discord spoiled the fellowship of the brothers. Abel had profited from the instruction of his father. He approached God with a lamb. Cain, the self-sufficient, was proud of his agriculture; he offered the work of his hands, and God was grieved. He said, "If thou doest well, shalt thou not be accepted? and if thou doest not well, the sin offering lieth at the door." But Cain's pride had been stung to fury. He was intensely proud of his best, and that best had been treated as though it were filthy rags. Why should he imitate his brother and take a lamb of the flock? And inbred sin asserted itself. This had not been possible in Adam's temptation, when the challenge had to come from an outside source. Alas, a sinful nature had been transmitted to Adam's son, and this occupied the throne of his affections. He needed a new heart.

The Staggering Tragedy.

Abel lay where he had fallen, and the ground was stained with blood. With arm uplifted, the slayer stood above his victim; then suddenly the colour drained from his cheeks. His face became ashen as he looked at his hand. What had he done? His brother was dead. He had murdered him. "And the Lord said unto Cain, Where is Abel thy brother? And he said, I know not: Am I my brother's keeper?" Poor Cain; he was struggling in the quicksands of sin, and every new movement increased his danger. Anger, jealousy, murder, lies— these were the milestones on his path to disaster. "And God said, What hast thou done? the voice of thy brother's blood crieth unto me from the ground. And now thou art cursed . . . And Cain went out from the presence of the Lord." Poor, poor man.

The home was silent; neither Adam nor Eve had anything to say. Memories hurt, as their sins came back to them. Eve's face was tear-stained; she had lost two boys —and she knew it was her own fault. Adam, strong and resourceful, yet pathetically incompetent to deal with this tragedy, remained morose and sad. He realized that "the way of transgressors is hard." Oh, that he had walked God's way!

ENOCH . . . who walked with God

(GENESIS 5:24)

They probably said he was a dreamer, for he was a man apart. It was not that he was unsociable or unapproachable, but he loved solitude. He was happy when he was alone. The frivolities of life did not attract him. His home was a place of dignity and peace, where the restful atmosphere suggested a sanctuary. There were moments when Enoch might easily have been its priest. The more hilarious of the population laughed at the old man, and said his ideas were stupid. Yet with calm assurance the saint went his way. Every day he walked in the countryside; and the more intimate of his friends knew that whenever he returned from such a walk, his face was alight with a strange emotion. His eyes reflected the glow of hidden fires. He was a man possessed. He loved walking—especially when he walked with God.

His Exquisite Fellowship

It would appear that God had re-discovered in Enoch that which had been lost in Adam. The Lord had walked with man in Eden, but sin had intervened and a most promising fellowship had been ruined. Now God had found a new companion. Enoch walked with God. We moderns liken progress to the growth of a child, and glibly say that a man must walk before he can run. God describes progress differently. The prophet Isaiah said, "They that wait upon the Lord shall renew their strength; *they shall mount up with wings* as eagles; *they shall run,* and not be weary; and *they shall walk* and not faint" (Isa. 40:31). When a man is first converted to God, the exuberance of spiritual youth will be wings upon which he will be carried to the skies. Then, as his experiences deepen, he will persistently run the race of life, and not be weary. Finally, he will walk at God's side. Excessive enthusiasm will not hasten his footsteps, nor will weariness slacken his pace, when God moves. Every day they will walk together. Enoch was one of the earliest men to attain to this degree of intimacy. *He walked with God.*

His Exceptional Faith

Walking with God means fellowship, and fellowship means conversation. The casual onlookers in the ancient world could not understand why the saint loved to steal away from the company of fellow men. Probably, had they secretly followed him, they would have questioned his sanity. He talked to an invisible companion. He told God all the secrets of his heart, and in return God revealed the plans of heaven. And slowly but surely, the old patriarch was instructed in matters beyond ordinary comprehension. His eyes became those of a seer, and from that day onward his voice rebuked the immorality of his generation. "And Enoch also, the seventh from Adam, prophesied . . . saying, Behold, the Lord cometh with ten thousands of his saints, to execute judgment upon all, and to convince all that are ungodly among them of all their ungodly deeds which they have ungodly committed . . ." (Jude 14, 15). God not only loved to walk with him; He trusted him with a great message. The preacher spoke with authority. He firmly believed what he said; he had received the information at first hand—he had walked with God.

His Eternal Fame

Day after day these two walked together, and perhaps even the angels marvelled. It was astounding that the Maker of heaven and earth should find delight in the company of a mere man. God loved Enoch, and His love was perfectly reciprocated. It was not a cause for amazement, therefore, when God invited Enoch to the eternal palace, and the invitation was gratefully accepted. They went home together. "By faith Enoch was translated that he should not see death; and was not found, because God had translated him: for before his translation he had this testimony, that he pleased God" (Heb. 11:5).

Probably the men of the city searched high and low for the missing preacher, and all kinds of rumours circulated concerning his strange disappearance. Yet they never found him, for they were unable to look in the right place. He was with God. And thus did God teach that, although a flaming sword blocked the way to the tree of life (Gen. 3:24), eternal life could still be a reality to all who walked with the Highest.

SARAH . . . who laughed at God

(GENESIS 18:9-15)

The Lord said unto Abraham, "Where is Sarah thy wife? And he said, Behold, in the tent. And the Lord said, I will certainly return unto thee according to the time of life; and, lo, Sarah thy wife shall have a son. And Sarah heard it in the tent door, which was behind him . . . Therefore Sarah laughed within herself, saying, After I am waxed old shall I have pleasure, my lord being old also? And the Lord said unto Abraham, Wherefore did Sarah laugh, saying, Shall I of a surety bear a child, which am old? Is anything too hard for the Lord?"

Thou shalt have a son, and shalt call his name Isaac

Poor Sarah! She could hardly believe her ears as she stood in the doorway of her tent. She was preparing her meal, but the apparent stupidity of the visitor had momentarily halted her activities. The words were still ringing in her ears—Sarah thy wife shall have a son! Amazed, she turned to look toward the strangers; and then her old shoulders silently shook. It was funny! The old lady tried hard to suppress her mirth, but the task was almost beyond her capabilities. She remembered the long years when the joys of motherhood had been denied, and the thought of nursing a baby now seemed ridiculous. Quietly she stole away, lest her silent laughter should become more boisterous; but even as her hands prepared the meal, her wrinkled face betrayed the humour of her soul. "Sarah thy wife shall have a son." What nonsense! The stranger had taken leave of his senses. Then suddenly she was afraid, for beyond the door a voice was asking, "Wherefore did Sarah laugh?" Abraham's eyes were wrathful as they silently searched for his wife. The Stranger was also displeased; and instantly embarrassed and guilty, Sarah said, "I laughed not." The Lord quietly replied, "Nay, but thou didst laugh," and Sarah was glad to escape from the tent. She realized now that God had spoken: but it was impossible—or was it?

Thou shalt have a son, and shalt call his name John

Poor Elisabeth! She was old and very disappointed. Her greatest longings had never been realized, for a baby's smiles had never thrilled her soul. The home had remained silent and empty. Her husband was a priest, and together they walked uprightly before the Lord. They had persistently presented their request for a child, but alas, their prayers had not been answered. " They had no child, because that Elisabeth was barren, and they both were now well stricken in years " (Luke 1:7). And while she sat at home patiently trusting in God, Zacharias went to follow his high and holy calling in the sanctuary. "And there appeared unto him an angel of the Lord standing on the right side of the altar of incense . . . and said, Fear not, Zacharias: for thy prayer is heard; and thy wife Elisabeth shall bear thee a son." He was astonished as he muttered to himself, " Impossible! I am an old man, and my wife is well stricken in years. A son! I'm dreaming." And if old Sarah could have been present, she would have laughed again: but this time her mirth would have been unrestrained. And when she recovered she would probably have looked at the priest and asked, " Didn't you hear about me? Priest, you have lots to learn." "And the angel answering said unto Zacharias . . . Behold thou shalt be dumb, and not able to speak . . . because thou believest not my words . . ."

Thou shalt have a Son, and shalt call his name Jesus

Poor Mary! She was greatly troubled, for the angel had said unto her, " Fear not, Mary: for thou hast found favour with God. And, behold, thou shalt conceive in thy womb, and bring forth a son, and shalt call his name Jesus . . . Then said Mary unto the angel, How shall this be, seeing I know not a man? And the angel answered and said unto her, The Holy Ghost shall come upon thee, and the power of the Highest shall overshadow thee: therefore also that holy thing which shall be born of thee shall be called the Son of God " (Luke 1:29-35). It was fantastic; it was impossible—or was it? Then Mary laughed, but hers was the laugh of faith. She said, " Behold the hand-maid of the Lord; be it unto me according to thy word." Her heart was filled with joy as she sang, " My soul doth magnify the Lord, and my spirit hath rejoiced in God my Saviour."

Sarah, Elisabeth and Zacharias, Mary. They all laughed; but she " who laughed last, laughed best."

ABRAHAM . . . who believed God

(GENESIS 22 : 5)

"It came to pass . . . that God did tempt Abraham, and said unto him . . . Take now thy son, thine only son Isaac, whom thou lovest, and get thee into the land of Moriah; and offer him there for a burnt offering upon one of the mountains which I will tell thee of. And Abraham rose up early in the morning . . . and went unto the place of which God had told him."

The Faith which brought Strength

"Abraham was an hundred years old, when his son Isaac was born unto him " (Gen. 21:5). When God sent Isaac, domestic difficulties soon upset the tranquillity of the home, and Abraham quickly recognized that two women cannot reign from the same throne. "Sarah said unto Abraham, Cast out this bondwoman and her son." And God said, "Let it not be grievous in thy sight . . . in all that Sarah hath said unto thee, hearken unto her voice; *for in Isaac shall thy seed be called*" (v. 12). Thus Abraham received a double blessing. The Lord gave immediate guidance concerning the domestic arrangements of the troubled home, and also a promise for the continuance of the race. Isaac was but a lad, yet his father knew the boy would marry and beget children, for the Lord had promised that "in Isaac shall thy seed be called." When God suggested that the child should be offered as a burnt offering, Abraham probably received the greatest shock of his life; but as he struggled with himself and with his problem, the memory of the promise reassured him. It was not possible for his child to die—and to remain in his grave—until he had become a father. "Then on the third day Abraham lifted up his eyes, and saw the place afar off. And Abraham said unto his young men, Abide ye here with the ass; and I and the lad will go yonder and worship, *and come again to you*." Abraham knew that if Isaac were slain, the Lord would raise him to life to fulfil the great promise. And if God did not permit the death of the boy, He would reveal a way out of the difficulty.

The Faith which brought a Substitute

"And Isaac spake unto Abraham his father, and said

9

. . . Behold the fire and the wood: but where is the lamb for a burnt-offering? And Abraham said, My son, God will provide himself a lamb for a burnt offering: so they went both of them together." Abraham was the man who believed God, and language seems inadequate to express the quality of his faith. Many years later the Lord Jesus said, " Your father Abraham rejoiced to see my day . . . and was glad." What did Abraham see? Should verse ei' it be printed like this: ". . . And Abraham said, My son, God will provide HIMSELF a lamb for a burnt offering"? If he saw Christ's day and was glad, did he also see that the Word would be made flesh and become the Lamb of God to take away the sins of the world? "And the angel of the Lord called unto him out of heaven . . . Lay not thy hand upon the lad, neither do thou anything unto him . . . And Abraham lifted up his eyes, and looked, and behold behind him a ram caught in a thicket by his horns." *By his horns.* Had the offering been caught by any other part of its body, parts of the fleece would have been left on the thorns, and the offering would not have been perfect in the sight of its Creator.

The Faith which brought Salvation

". . . And Abraham went and took the ram, and offered him up for a burnt-offering in the stead of his son." The lad was removed from the altar; the ram took his place, and through that ancient act of substitution, one of the earliest Gospel types was presented to the world. As Isaac returned to his home, he realized that an offering had died in his stead. And every day, Abraham watched his son growing on toward manhood. "And the angel of the Lord called unto Abraham out of heaven the second time, and said, By myself have I sworn, saith the Lord, for because thou hast done this thing . . . that in blessing I will bless thee, and in multiplying I will multiply thy seed as the stars of the heaven, and as the sand which is upon the seashore . . . And in thy seed shall all the nations of the earth be blessed; because thou hast obeyed my voice " (Gen. 22:15-18).

> Oh, help me then to understand
> How great was thy rich grace;
> I should have died upon that cross,
> But Thou didst take my place.

REBEKAH . . . who loved one she had never seen
(Genesis 24:58-67)

This is one of the most suggestive of the Old Testament stories, and all evangelistic preachers will discover a gold-mine of truth in its details. It is the account of a father who planned a marriage for his son—his well-beloved son. It tells of the trustworthy servant who was authorized to seek a bride for Isaac. It describes the invitation given to a charming young woman, and how she learned to love someone whom she had never seen. This remarkable episode clearly demonstrates that the divine Author was able to embody in ancient stories glimpses of eternal things yet to be revealed to man.

A Great Request

"Abraham was old, and well stricken in age . . . and he said unto his eldest servant . . . go unto my country, and to my kindred, and take a wife unto my son Isaac . . . And the servant took ten camels . . . and went to Mesopotamia, unto the city of Nahor " (Gen. 24:1-10). And even before he reached his destination, the Lord had prepared the way. Prayers were answered, and ultimately the man realized that the desired maiden stood before him. When he had been introduced to her family, he revealed to them the nature of his mission, and then calmly awaited their reactions. Rebekah listened to every word, and quietly noted every detail concerning the man to whom she would be betrothed. She had never seen him; she knew little about him; yet she was singularly attracted by the remarkable testimony of this stranger. His quiet assurance, his deep convictions, his smiling eyes, all impressed her soul; and when she saw the presents which he offered, her heart thrilled. Many years later, the Lord Jesus said, " Howbeit when he, the Spirit of truth, is come, he will guide you into all truth . . . He shall glorify me: for he shall receive of mine, *and shall shew it unto you*" (John 16:13-15).

A Gracious Response

"And they said, We will call the damsel, and enquire at her mouth. And they called Rebekah, and said unto her, Wilt thou go with this man?   And she said, I will go "

(Gen. 24:57-58). Three outstanding features are revealed in Rebekah's answer. (i) *Love responding.* It seemed ridiculous that she should consent to marry one whom she had never seen; the future might be filled with unhappiness. She had no guide but the witness of this stranger; yet his testimony awakened a response in her heart. (ii) *Love renouncing.* "And her brother and her mother said, Let the damsel abide with us a few days, at the least ten; after that she shall go. And the servant said unto them, Hinder me not . . . send me away that I may go to my master." And when appeal was made to the listening daughter, Rebekah supported his request. She became one of the select company who, for the master's sake, forsook houses, brethren, sisters, father, and mother, and in the end received a hundredfold and life everlasting (see Matt. 19:29). (iii) *Love rejoicing.* "And Rebekah arose, and her damsels, and they rode upon the camels, and followed the man: and the servant took Rebekah, and went his way." And as her dreamy eyes looked into the unknown, her heart was singing.

A Glorious Reward

"And Isaac went out to meditate in the field at eventide: and he lifted up his eyes, and saw, and, behold, the camels were coming . . . And when Rebekah saw Isaac, she lighted off her camel. For she had said unto the servant, What man is this that walketh in the field to meet us? And the servant had said, It is my master . . . And Isaac brought her into his mother Sarah's tent, and took Rebekah and she became his wife; and he loved her . . ." And when Isaac intreated the Lord for his wife, God graciously heard his requests, and the joy of motherhood became a reality in the life of this brave woman (see Gen. 25:21). Undoubtedly she often remembered the eventful moments when the strange challenge reached her, but never once had she cause to regret the response made when she left all and followed him.

Centuries later, the apostle Peter wrote, "Jesus Christ: Whom having not seen, ye love; in whom, though now ye see him not, yet believing, ye rejoice with joy unspeakable and full of glory" (1 Pet. 1:7, 8). Rebekah would have loved to listen as Simon Peter preached the Gospel. He would have been telling her story!

JACOB . . . who saw a ladder he couldn't climb

(GENESIS 28:12)

Things had not worked out according to plan, and Jacob was beginning to feel miserable. His home, his friends, and most of all, his mother, to whom he was devoted, had all been left behind. Weary, and pathetically alone, he journeyed into the wilderness; for Isaac his father had said unto him, "Arise, go to Padan-aram, to the house of Bethuel thy mother's father; and take thee a wife from thence of the daughters of Laban thy mother's brother . . . And he took of the stones of that place, and put them for his pillows, and lay down in that place to sleep" (Gen. 28:2-11).

God's Gracious Love—Sublime

As weariness overcame him, Jacob forgot the hardness of his pillow and slept; and suddenly the stillness of the night became alive with drama. "And he dreamed, and behold a ladder set up on the earth, and the top of it reached to heaven: and behold the angels of God ascending and descending upon it. And, behold, the Lord stood above it, and said, I am the Lord God of Abraham thy father, and the God of Isaac: the land whereon thou liest, to thee will I give it, and to thy seed" (vv. 12, 13). Enthralled, and greatly afraid, the fugitive watched the parade of angels; and the more he saw, the more he trembled. Probably he was too overcome to realize the greatness of divine affection. The Lord did not claim to be Jacob's God, for that important matter had still to be decided. Yet He was the God of Abraham and Isaac, and to these patriarchs He had given covenant promises. He had promised to be with their seed in all places whithersoever they went, and in spite of the lamentable delinquency of this deceitful sinner, God was still true to His covenant.

God's Great Ladder—Sufficient

". . . and behold a ladder set up on the earth, and the top of it reached to heaven." Perhaps Jacob recognized that the company on the ladder was very select, for none but angels ascended and descended. Yet God was demonstrating that there was a way by which entrance could be made into His presence. It is interesting to notice that the angels were first *ascending* the ladder. One would expect that the order would have been reversed. This ladder was not let down from heaven—*it was set up on the earth.* The angels were not descending and then ascending again. They were first going into the presence of God, and then ultimately returning to earth. It might be that Hebrews 1:14 can explain the ancient problem. "Are they (the angels) not all ministering spirits, sent forth to minister for them who shall be heirs of salvation? " The angels are with us, guarding, guiding, and assisting the saints. The ladder might easily be the ladder of prayer, upon which they carry our petitions to the throne of grace, and on which they return with the answers.

God's Guilty Listener—Startled

"And Jacob was afraid, and said, How dreadful is this place! this is none other but the house of God, and this is the gate of heaven " (v. 17). Not even the magnificent promise of God's help could remove the dread from his soul. He was desperately guilty, and no man may be at home in God's presence unless pardoning grace has removed the stains from his conscience. Poor Jacob was terrified, and was glad to continue his journey. Yet in all the strange vicissitudes of his life, God never forsook him; and when these early lessons had been fully learned, when he had wrestled and prevailed with the Lord at Peniel, he discovered that God's great ladder was indeed a bright and a glorious reality. Perhaps he would have understood far more had he been able to hear the words of the Saviour, for in after days Christ likened the ladder to Himself. "And Jesus said unto Nathaniel, Verily, verily, I say unto you, Hereafter ye shall see heaven opened, and the angels of God ascending and descending upon the Son of man " (John 1:51). And probably Jacob would have understood even more had he been able to sing with the hymnist—

> Oh, safe and happy shelter!
> Oh, refuge tried and sweet!
> Oh, trysting place where heaven's love
> And heaven's justice meet!
> As to the holy patriarch
> That wondrous dream was given,
> So seems my Saviour's cross to me
> A ladder up to heaven.

THE CREATOR . . . who altered the calendar

(EXODUS 12:2)

A new year is always a time of new beginnings. The trials and difficulties of the past are left behind, and the future seems bright with prospect and hope. Then, men go forth with new ambitions, determined to reach heights of success unattained in the previous year. Such an occasion is a time of joy among all people. Yet only once in history did a new year arrive unexpectedly. The Book of Exodus tells of a time when God gave His unprecedented command to begin a new year even before the old year had expired. If we may be permitted to use the names of our calendar months, then the time might have been the middle of August when the Lord said, "Let this day be January the first." Such a procedure had been unknown in the history of the human race, and the text invites investigation.

The New Year of Redemption

"And the Lord spake unto Moses and Aaron in the land of Egypt, saying, This month shall be unto you the beginning of months: it shall be the first month of the year unto you. Speak ye unto all the congregation of Israel, saying, In the tenth day of this month, they shall take to them every man a lamb, according to the house of their fathers, a lamb for an house . . . Your lamb shall be without blemish . . . and the whole congregation of Israel shall kill it in the evening. And they shall take of the blood and strike it on the two side posts and on the upper door post of the houses . . . For I will pass through the land of Egypt this night, and will smite all the firstborn in the land of Egypt . . . and when I see the blood, I will pass over you, and the plague shall not be upon you to destroy you, when I smite the land of Egypt. And this day shall be unto you for a memorial; and ye shall keep it a feast to the Lord throughout your generations; ye shall keep it a feast by an ordinance for ever" (Ex. 12: 1-14).

This act of God in altering the calendar was truly prophetic. Here we find the veiled foreshadowings of that greater experience, when the old year of bondage to sin suddenly terminates. Here we see the type of that

15

supreme moment when, through the sacrifice of the Lamb of God, a new experience is made possible for sinners. The Lord Jesus said to Nicodemus, " Marvel not that I said unto thee, Ye must be born again," and when the ruler of the synagogue replied by asking, " How can these things be?" Christ answered, "As Moses lifted up the serpent in the wilderness, even so must the Son of man be lifted up." Redemption comes through the cross, and man's new beginning comes through redemption.

The New Year of Sanctification

"And the Lord spake unto Moses, saying, On the first day of the first month shalt thou set up the tabernacle of the tent of the congregation . . . *And it came to pass in the first month in the second year, on the first day of the month,* that the tabernacle was reared up . . . Then a cloud covered the tent of the congregation, and the glory of the Lord filled the tabernacle. And when the cloud was taken up . . the children of Israel went onward in all their journeys: but if the cloud were not taken up, then they journeyed not until the day that it was taken up. For the cloud of the Lord was upon the tabernacle by day, and fire was on it by night, in the sight of all the house of Israel, throughout all their journeys " (Ex. 40). It would seem, from the sacred account, that Israel's second new year was even greater than the first. In the former, God came down to redeem His people; in the latter, He came down to live among His people. He redeemed them in order to have fellowship with them, and His greatest desires were unfulfilled until the cloud of His presence rested upon the sanctuary. And here again we find the suggestions of New Testament truth. The story of the cross reveals God's redemption of man; the story of Pentecost tells how the Holy Spirit seeks to live in the hearts of all believers. Once again it is a new beginning. It is possible to be a Christian and not be filled with the Holy Spirit. Conversion depends upon my faith in the blood of the Lamb; holiness depends upon my determination to crucify all that pertains to the flesh. If the Lord is to set up His tabernacle in my territory, I must clear the building site of all rubbish.

MOSES . . . and his recurring challenge

(Exodus 32:26)

The camp of Israel was in an uproar, and the noise of the ribald shoutings echoed far up the mountain side. Around the golden calf naked men and women heedlessly danced in reckless abandon. High on the hillside, Moses listened and said to his servant Joshua, " It is not the voice of them that shout for mastery, neither is it the voice of them that cry for being overcome: but the noise of them that sing do I hear. And it came to pass as soon as Moses came nigh unto the camp, that he saw the calf, and the dancing: and Moses' anger waxed hot . . . And when Moses saw that the people were naked . . . he stood in the gate of the camp, and said, Who is on the Lord's side? let him come unto me " (Ex. 32:18-26).

The Challenge of Moses

And immediately all the sons of Levi moved toward their revered leader. "And he said unto them, Thus saith the Lord God of Israel, Put every man his sword by his side, and go in and out from gate to gate throughout the camp, and slay every man his brother, and every man his companion, and every man his neighbour. And the children of Levi did according to the word of Moses " (vv. 27, 28). Thus ended one of the most tragic days in Israel; but before the shadows finally obliterated the scene, certain things had become evident. (i) The people who had sinned had not done so ignorantly. The absence of Moses did not provide an adequate excuse for wilful disobedience. (ii) The people who had abstained had not done so accidentally. To refuse to conform to the popular idea was to invite persecution. Such action demanded great courage. (iii) The execution of justice was not done sentimentally. Men were commanded to slay members of their own families. True religion demands that God be first in all matters. The challenge of Moses split the camp into two sections.

The Challenge of Jehu

An ominous sombre silence had settled on the city; the streets were empty; it was the calm before the storm. The fiery captain Jehu had developed a great hatred of idolatry, and the worshippers of Baal were frightened. Jezebel remained in her palace, and smiled. Other men had found her charms to be irresistible; Jehu should be no exception to the rule. "And when Jehu was come to Jezreel, Jezebel heard of it; and she painted her face, and tired her head, and looked out at a window." Her bewitching face and coquettish manners were meant to ensnare the brave reformer; but he refused to be deceived. His challenging cry rang through the street: "Who is on my side? who? And there looked out to him two or three eunuchs. And he said, Throw her down . . . and he trode her under foot" (2 Kings 9:30-33). And once again three things became evident. (i) No man can be on two sides at the same time. (ii) No man can be truly on God's side and remain hidden. (iii) No man can be truly on God's side unless he openly fights against evil. A pretty face can never disguise a foul heart when a man of God is the detective!

The Challenge of Christ

Ecclesiastical arrogance began to appear when John said unto Jesus, "Master, we saw one casting out devils in thy name, and he followeth not us: and we forbad him, because he followeth not us" (Mark 9:38). Who was the unknown healer? That he knew and preached the correct message no one can doubt, but the disciples were unduly disturbed because he had "not joined their church." He was an upstart! It was like his cheek to imitate people in holy orders! Master, we told him to stop! "But Jesus said, Forbid him not: for there is no man who shall do a miracle in my name, that can lightly speak evil of me. For he that is not against me is on our part" (vv. 39, 40). Let us consider three vital features. (i) The followers of Christ are never confined to a single select band. (ii) An unashamed confession of Christ is the hallmark of true devotion. (iii) The true follower of Christ will be loyal even when his Lord is apparently absent. We are glad the Lord dealt with his belligerent disciples, for true ordination comes from God. Sometimes He uses the well-known ministers—the Peters and Johns of His followers; and sometimes He uses the unknown fellow who lives in the other street. Does it matter—so long as souls are healed in the Name of Jesus?

THE WATERS OF MARAH . . . and a study in trees

(Exodus 15:22-25)

" He cried unto the Lord; *and the Lord shewed him a tree* . . ." The Marked New Testament has always attracted me, for the words of the Saviour printed in red type indicate messages of unusual importance. I have often said I would like to treat the entire Bible in similar manner, for here and there in the Scriptures we find statements of superlative interest. The text, " and the Lord shewed him a tree," is a striking example of that fact. The Cross may be seen almost anywhere in the Bible.

The Tree in the Garden of Eden

"And the Lord God planted a garden eastward in Eden . . . And out of the ground made the Lord God to grow every tree that is pleasant . . . *the tree of life* also in the midst of the garden, and the tree of the knowledge of good and evil " (Gen. 2:8-9). It seems unfortunate that the theological emphasis has been on the second tree, and that the more important of the two trees, the tree of life, has been ignored. God created a perfect man, but Adam had to choose to conform to the divine will. When he disobeyed, sin entered his soul; had he been a wiser man and taken of the tree of life, he would have become " a partaker of the divine nature " (see Gen. 3:22-24). Thus even in the earliest days of human history, God suggested that eternal life would be irrevocably linked with a sinner's intelligent approach to a *tree*.

The Tree at the Waters of Marah

" So Moses brought Israel from the Red sea, and they went out into the wilderness of Shur; and they went three days in the wilderness, and found no water. And when they came to Marah, they could not drink of the waters of Marah, for they were bitter " (Ex. 15:22, 23). The situation was rapidly deteriorating when Moses desperately cried unto the Lord, and was shewn a tree. Possibly the scoffers in Israel laughed, but their scorn disappeared when God used that tree to bring living waters to their parched and complaining lips.

The Tree and the Serpent of Brass

The children of Israel were dying when, in answer to

the prayer of Moses, God said, " Make thee a fiery serpent, and set it upon a pole: and it shall come to pass that every one that is bitten, when he looketh upon it, shall live " (Num. 21:8). Centuries later the Lord Jesus said, "And as Moses lifted up the serpent in the wilderness, even so must the Son of man be lifted up: that whosoever believeth in him should not perish, but have everlasting life " (John 3:14-15).

The Tree and the Lost Axe-Head

The servants of Elisha were engaged in building operations when disaster fell upon the activities of one energetic young man. His " axe-head fell into the water: and he cried, and said, Alas, master! for it was borrowed. And the man of God said, Where fell it? And he shewed him the place. And he cut down a stick, and cast it in thither; and the iron did swim. Therefore said he, Take it up to thee. And he put out his hand and took it " (2 Kings 6:5-7). Everyone who has seen dead sinners raised to newness of life will rejoice, for— Is anything too hard for the power of Calvary's cross?

The Tree and the Balm of Gilead

The forests of Gilead were famous throughout the ancient world. The trees produced a substance rich in medicinal quality, and " the balm of Gilead " was in world-wide demand. It was this fact which led the prophet of God to ask, " Is there no balm in Gilead? " (Jer. 8:22). Surely, a world was being prepared for the time when healing virtues would stream from the cross of Calvary; when people of many nations would be able to " come and buy . . . without money and without price " (Isa. 55:1).

The Tree in the Teaching of Christ

" From that time forth began Jesus to shew unto his disciples, how that he must go unto Jerusalem, and suffer many things of the elders and chief priests and scribes, and be killed, and be raised again the third day " (Matt. 16:21). The tree of life stood in the midst of the garden of Eden; the tree of grace stands in the centre of the will of God. At the former, Adam might have found life; at the latter, we have found life more abundant.

> I take, O Cross, thy shadow
> For my abiding place.

RAHAB . . . whose life hung by a thread
(JOSHUA 2:18-19)

The Bible has given to us several facts concerning the story of Rahab the harlot, and it is a little unfortunate that some of these are unknown to the casual reader. The fact that this remarkable woman was a great sinner has overshadowed all else, and in speaking of her scarlet thread, we have forgotten that this incident was only the beginning of a chain of events which, to say the least, is one of the most romantic stories of the Scriptures. Rahab the harlot, the great sinner, became one of the most dignified ladies in Israel.

The New Hope

The fear of the children of Israel had fallen upon Jericho, and the " city was straitly shut up." Faces were strained, and almost hourly the king and his counsellors met to discuss the threatened invasion. A state of emergency had been declared, and the future of Jericho seemed ominous. In common with all other places, the harlot's house on the wall was a place of dread. When she saw the two strangers furtively stealing through the gloom, she guessed that they were spies from Israel, and immediately became exceedingly resourceful. At the risk of her life she safeguarded the men, and received from them the promise of salvation. The scarlet thread hanging from the window would be a guarantee of protection. She believed the message, and would not have sold that thread for all the money in Jericho.

The New Heart

"And Joshua saved Rahab the harlot alive, and her father's household, and all that she had; *and she dwelleth in Israel even unto this day;* because she hid the messengers which Joshua sent to spy out Jericho " (Josh. 6:25). Somewhere among the people of the Lord her family erected a new home, and a remarkable change came over the immoral woman. She listened to new conversations, and watched with shining eyes the ceremonial sacrifices, and slowly but surely she desired to leave her evil ways. It would not be difficult for Rahab to do this, for her change of heart helped her to renounce her former habits.

The New Home

Noble resolves changed her manner of living, and a new radiance shone upon her countenance. Probably she had always been an attractive woman, but now a singular beauty became apparent to everyone. It was not a cause for amazement when Salmon sought her in marriage. Perhaps this young man had been one of the original spies, and had never forgotten the kindness of this charming young woman. The new Rahab accepted her suitor, and somewhere in Israel another home came into being. The past failings were forgotten; happiness flooded the two young hearts; and when God blessed their home by sending a baby boy, their cup of joy was filled to the brim. The proud parents adored their son, and called him Booz (Matt. 1:5). Sometimes in the cool of the evening the young mother would nurse her child, and as his starry eyes looked into her face, she sang her lullabies and quietly thanked God.

The New Happiness

The years passed by, and Rahab became a distinguished old lady of Israel. She enjoyed the respect of all people, and her son Booz was destined to become famous. "And Naomi had a kinsman of her husband's, a mighty man of wealth, of the family of Elimelech; and his name was Boaz" (Ruth 2:1). If the great old lady saw the return of Naomi from Moab, she witnessed the unfolding of the greatest drama of her life. Her boy fell in love with the Moabite maiden Ruth, and ultimately married her. Ruth's new mother-in-law was Rahab, whose memory brought back many thoughts of bygone experiences. When Rahab looked into the eyes of her daughter-in-law, she remembered that she also had been a Gentile who had been rescued and brought into the fellowship of God's people. And if she lived to see the birth of her grandchild Obed, she was one of the happiest women in Israel. "And they called his name Obed: he is the father of Jesse, the father of David" (Ruth 4:17).

ACHAN . . . who paralysed an Army

(JOSHUA 7:1-26)

The children of Israel were jubilant; the crashing of Jericho's walls still sounded in their ears. Some of the people had been a little anxious, for the Canaanite stronghold had seemed to be impregnable. When Israel marched around the city, their actions bordered on the ludicrous; yet the face of the young leader shone with the light of absolute assurance. He had bowed before the Captain of the Lord's hosts, and had received his orders. His faith had been rewarded when the piercing notes of the trumpeters were drowned in the thunderous collapse of the walls. Then the people had taken the city, and their last vestiges of doubt completely vanished. Their God was truly omnipotent. When they had finally consolidated their position, they prepared for a further advance and, behold, the little town of Ai stood in their path. It was insignificant; it was beneath their dignity to devote their newly acquired strength to the elimination of such a midget!

A Startling Defeat

" So there went up thither of the people about three thousand men: and they fled before the men of Ai. And the men of Ai smote of them about thirty and six men, for they chased them from before the gate even unto Shebarim, and smote them in the going down: wherefore the hearts of the people melted, and became as water. And Joshua rent his clothes, and . . . said, Alas, O Lord God . . ." (vv. 4-7). And in the hours that followed, the nation's joys were turned to mourning, and the pessimistic people forgot their earlier victory and longed to be " back on the other side of Jordan." "And the Lord said unto Joshua, Get thee up; wherefore liest thou thus upon thy face? Israel hath sinned . . ." (vv. 10, 11). God is no respecter of persons. Sin is still sin, even when it is found in the hearts of God's own people. No man can be sure of victory in spiritual warfare unless he maintains the purity of his own soul. One Achan can ruin the greatest spiritual enterprise.

A Surprising Discovery

And the Lord said, " Up, sanctify the people, and say,

Sanctify yourselves against tomorrow: for thus saith the Lord God of Israel, There is an accursed thing in the midst of thee, O Israel" (v. 13). When the lots were cast, "Achan . . . was taken. And Joshua said, My son, give, I pray thee, glory to the Lord God of Israel, and make confession unto him, and tell me now what thou hast done; hide it not from me. And Achan answered Joshua, and said, Indeed I have sinned against the Lord God" (vv. 18-20). Then followed the account of his confiscating some of the prohibited things of Jericho. A beautiful Babylonian garment, two hundred shekels of silver, and a wedge of gold had been hidden in his tent. He had looked all around before he hid the treasures, to make sure that no one was watching; but alas, he forgot to look up. Achan's sin had paralysed the army, and divine blessing had been withheld from the nation. (i) *God's people are ONE people.* As individual members we are united in the fellowship of one body. Achan's personal sin affected the entire nation. (ii) *God's perception is intensely keen.* He hates sin, particularly when it is hidden. Achan sinned when he took the articles, but he became a hypocrite when he buried them. (iii) *God's pleasure is discriminative.* With Him we succeed; without Him we fail.

A Sad Death

"And Joshua, and all Israel with him, took Achan . . . and the silver, and the garment, and the wedge of gold . . . And all Israel stoned him with stones" (vv. 24, 25). Poor man! Are we being too sentimental when we feel sorry for him? He lived in an age of law, when men had to be taught the hatefulness of sin; and alas, his secret sin had already sent thirty-six Israelites to their graves. Judgment removed him from the camp of Israel. How thankful we should be that, in the fullness of time, God found another way of removing iniquity. The Lord Jesus made Himself personally responsible for the sins of innumerable Achans—He died that they might be forgiven. Gratitude should prevent any Achan-like sins remaining in our hearts. No Ai will thwart us, and no enemy overcome us if we keep our hands and hearts clean.

"Be ye clean, that bear the vessels of the Lord" (Isa. 52:11).

ADONI-BEZEK . . . the toe and thumb specialist

(JUDGES 1 : 5-7)

He was a foul unmitigated scoundrel, a blot on the society of his day, and a shameful law unto himself. His weird eccentricities were widely known, and probably many people said he was mentally unbalanced. Yet his evil deeds continued unchecked, and his name became increasingly infamous throughout the land. He loved to dethrone and mutilate kings. Then with grim delight he watched and laughed as his unfortunate captives " gleaned " at his table.

A Royal Collection

To all but a semi-maniac, the sights in the palace dining room would have been nauseating. Seventy kings crouched against the walls hopefully watching a gluttonous monarch. The presence of the guards was a guarantee against insurrection, for their long whips were ready to administer instant punishment to any man who felt disposed to rebel against his treatment. Hungry eyes furtively watched the table, and as the detestable king threw pieces of food to the floor, the starving men fought like jackals for the portions, and all the while the mocking laughter of the watching scoundrel echoed through the room. Even the guards enjoyed the fun as the desperate men rolled over each other in the mad scramble for food. Adoni-bezek, the Canaanite king, was able to say, " Threescore and ten kings, having their thumbs and their great toes cut off, gleaned their meat under my table." Without thumbs, their hands had become claws; and without their big toes, their sense of balance had been impaired. To watch these starving men desperately struggling for survival was highly amusing, and the chief among the sordid onlookers was Adoni-bezek himself.

A Rebuking Conscience

It was almost inconceivable that he should ever feel concerned about the shamefulness of his conduct. His behaviour suggested that he had never heard of God, and yet this was not so. Archaeological discoveries have proved that the Canaanites spoke a language similar to that in use among the Hebrews, and it is therefore most

<font>25</font>

likely that the people of the land were acquainted with the earliest forms of religion. We do not know the degree of Adoni-bezek's knowledge, but it is truly significant that from his own lips came the confession that God had watched the revolting displays in the palace. Such a revelation could hardly have taken place in a moment. The fires of conscience had not been completely extinguished; they had slowly but unmistakably smouldered in his mind. Yet during all the years of savage enjoyment, this arrogant man had rudely thrust aside any attempt of God's Spirit to lead him into nobler avenues of life and service. He was fascinated by his cruel hobby; he revelled in the sense of his own indisputable superiority, and neither religion nor ethics should rob him of this source of pleasure. Nevertheless the pin-pricks of conscience made themselves felt, and when grim retribution eventually overtook the guilty man, his first words spoke of God.

A Remarkable Confession

"And Judah went up; and the Lord delivered the Canaanites and the Perizzites into their hand: and they slew of them in Bezek ten thousand men. And they found Adoni-bezek in Bezek, and they fought against him . . . But Adoni-bezek fled; and they pursued after him, and caught him, and cut off his thumbs and his great toes. And Adoni-bezek said, Threescore and ten kings having their thumbs and their great toes cut off, gleaned their meat under my table: *as I have done, so God hath requited me.*" Then he discovered that the opportunity to repent had vanished. He had lived either in ignorance or open indifference of one of the greatest principles of life and law. " Be not deceived; God is not mocked: for whatsoever a man soweth, that shall he also reap. For he that soweth to his flesh shall of the flesh reap corruption: but he that soweth to the Spirit shall of the Spirit reap life everlasting " (Gal. 6:7-8). And it would seem that in this important matter, Adoni-bezek was not alone. " And they brought him to Jerusalem, and there he died." Before the throne of God he would be without excuse; a poor, destitute, bankrupt soul, with no friend—no hope— no Saviour. He had deliberately closed his eyes to the requirements of moral and spiritual law, and his ultimate fate should be a warning to us all.

GIDEON . . . and his strange way of fighting a battle

(JUDGES 7:20)

The man seemed stupified. He could hardly believe his eyes. The vandalism of a religious fanatic had smashed the altar of Baal, and the evidence of a furious onslaught lay all around in the dust. The onlooker stood as though turned to stone, and in those moments of horror he saw also the other altar which had been erected alongside the fallen idol. Suddenly his wild cries rang through the street, and almost immediately his fellow citizens came running to the scene of the commotion. Stunned and bewildered, they stared at the overturned idol, and then angrily demanded the name of the prowling iconoclast. Someone mentioned Gideon, the son of Joash, and immediately the infuriated mob surged toward the well-known homestead. "Then the men of the city said unto Joash, Bring out thy son, that he may die: because he hath cast down the altar of Baal . . . And Joash said unto all them that stood against him, Will ye plead for Baal? . . . If he be a god, let him plead for himself" (Judges 6:30, 31). And the calm demeanour of the old man restrained the angry people, and ultimately prepared the way for the deliverance of the nation. The Spirit of the Lord came upon Gideon; the men of Israel rallied to his standard, and after long years of cruel bondage, the might of the enemy was challenged.

Faith Which Startled

Gideon's first attack against idolatry was made under cover of darkness, but subsequent events encouraged confidence, and finally he became a mighty man of faith. His army was systematically reduced in size until the entire enterprise bordered on the ludicrous. With three hundred followers, this dauntless man would challenge a host whose "camels were without number, as the sand by the seaside for multitude" (7:12). Stealthily the intrepid warriors crept to their allocated positions, and holding their meagre equipment in their hands, they awaited their leader's signal. Unsuspecting and drunken, the enemy sprawled all over the valley as Gideon quietly surveyed the scene. Then the silence of the night was shattered as three hundred men smashed their earthen pitchers. Amid the peacefulness of the night, the noise resembled an ominous thunderclap from another world. Rampaging fears struck terror in the hearts of the awakening Midianites, and rushing from their tents, they drew their swords and frantically stabbed into the darkness.

Faith Which Shone

When the terrified men saw lights dancing around their camp, their last vestiges of courage fled. Gideon had given lamps to every man, with instructions that these should be hidden within the earthen pitchers until the vessels had been destroyed. Then "the men held their lamps in their left hands, and the trumpets in their right hands" (7:20). Exultant faith filled their hearts, and three hundred pairs of eyes seemed balls of fire on that night of vengeance. Again and again their wild cries echoed through the night—"The sword of the Lord and of Gideon." Then came the sounds of three hundred trumpets—an accelerated symphony of praise which reached even to heaven.

Faith Which Sang

"And the three hundred blew the trumpets, and the Lord set every man's sword against his fellow" (v. 22). Then Israel's faith sang, for it became evident that the haunting days of Midianite oppression had gone for ever. Never again would foul invaders pillage the land, burn their crops, and reduce Israel to starvation. God had truly visited His people. An earthen pitcher! A shining lamp! A trumpet! What strange weapons of war; yet these have always been outstanding weapons in God's armoury. In order to express the greatness of his message, Paul used similar phraseology. He believed that the outshining of the light of the indwelling Spirit was dependent upon the breaking—or shall we say, the crucifixion—of the human vessel. He said, "We have this treasure in earthen vessels" (2 Cor. 4:7). His identification with Christ in death and resurrection led to Pentecost, where the lips of the saint could be placed on the trumpet, and the note of victory could echo through the darkness of sin's battlefield. Gideon and Paul would have been very happy to compare notes on military strategy.

JEPHTHAH . . . who made a vow and kept it
(JUDGES 11:30-39)

Jephthah was a Gileadite, and fire ran in his veins. He belonged to Elijah's country. The keen hillside winds blew upon his face; his eyes reflected the blue of God's heaven; his spirit was as formidable as the mountains upon which he roamed. He possessed great strength and glorious restraint—a rare combination indeed. His birth certificate was non-existent, and his illegitimate entry into the family circle constantly grieved his sensitive soul. When his brethren drove him away from home, the mighty warrior went without a protest. He was conquered not by their strength, but by his own shame. He was a rare bloom which had arisen from the muddy depths of human depravity—but he *was* a rare bloom for all that.

A Great Vow

Somewhere in the land of Tob, this valiant fighter built his new home, and commenced life all over again. He missed his kinsfolk; he yearned for the open hills of Gilead: but it was better to live alone than to live in strife. Besides, he had his daughter—a princess in his simple palace. And then one day a deputation arrived from Gilead. The anxious elders acquainted Jephthah with their tale of woe, and earnestly solicited his help. The Ammonites were threatening war, and Israel had no leader. Jephthah, please come and help us! "And Jephthah said unto the elders of Gilead, Did not ye hate me, and expel me out of my father's house? and why are ye come to me now when ye are in distress? " (Judges 11:7). Responding to their appeal for help, and accepting their offer of leadership, he went forth to battle. "And Jephthah vowed a vow unto the Lord, and said, If thou shalt without fail deliver the children of Ammon into my hands, then it shall be that whatsoever cometh forth of the doors of my house to meet me, when I return in peace from the children of Ammon, shall surely be the Lord's, and I will offer it up for a burnt offering " (vv. 30, 31).

A Glorious Victory

He went forth in the name of the Lord, and his enemies were subdued before him. Flushed with a glorious triumph, he returned to his home, "and, behold, his daughter came out to meet him with timbrels and dances: and she was his only child; beside her he had neither son nor daughter. And it came to pass when he saw her, that he rent his clothes, and said, Alas, my daughter!" He had been fighting battles all day, but the greatest conflict was fought in that evening hour. The conquest of the Ammonites had been child's play compared with the conquest of self. Perhaps we shall never realize what it cost this poor man before he succeeded in "crucifying the flesh with the affections thereof." Various explanations have been given in regard to the fulfilment of this vow. Some maintain that the girl was offered a living sacrifice upon the altar; others have stressed the fact that in this case it was more an offering or a vow of celibacy— that the girl's life was surrendered for exclusive service in the sanctuary. Yet, whichever interpretation may be correct, the fact remains that the sacrifice hurt. Nevertheless, although sorrow ravaged his heart, Jephthah honoured his obligations, It is easy to criticize the apparent rashness of his vow, for if we are in the habit of breaking our vows, the story of his faithfulness will be a thorn in our rebellious flesh.

A Girl's Virtue

"And she said unto him . . . do to me according to that which hath proceeded out of thy mouth" (vv. 36-39). Like father—like daughter. Surely she was a princess of heaven. The only way to assess her greatness is to place her alongside modern people. Utterly selfless, she recognized that the supreme achievement in life was to do the will of God. If she died in sacrifice, then her eyes reflected the glow of hidden fires of devotion. If her remaining days were spent in the exclusive service of the house of God, then her presence graced the sanctuary. Her father was left alone—pitifully alone; and within six years he was dead. Probably he broke his heart. He was a man of iron; a man of flame; undaunted, unselfish, completely reliable and trustworthy. What might God do today if His servants were men and women of this calibre?

THE PRIEST OF GOD . . . who ministered in
a heathen temple

" Micah had an house of gods, and made an ephod . . ."
(Judges 17:5, 6). Yes, the idolater was very proud of his
temple, and his fanatical eyes shone with delight when he
surveyed his collection of gods. " And there was a young
man out of Beth-lehem-judah, one of the family of
Judah, who was a Levite . . . and he came to mount
Ephraim to the house of Micah, as he journeyed . . . And
Micah said unto him, Dwell with me, and be unto me
a father and a priest, and I will give thee ten shekels of
silver by the year, and a suit of apparel, and thy victuals.
So the Levite went in " (vv. 7-10).

An Unemployed Priest—Why?

He belonged to the Levites—the people responsible for
the upkeep and the services of the sanctuary at Shiloh.
Had he followed the example of his fellow Levites, he
would have been busy in the service of God; but something had interfered with his normal course of duty.
What was it? (i) *Had he sinned?* And as a result had
he been banished from the ministry of God's house? (ii)
Had he been frustrated in his ambitions? Had he served
in a minor position, and longed for a more important and
a more remunerative task? (iii) *Had he been restless?*
Had the work in God's house bored him, and had he
seized the first opportunity to leave the district? Thus
he forsook his task and departed—an unemployed priest
who had lost both the desire and the opportunity of
serving in holy things.

An Unfaithful Priest—Why?

" And the Levite was content to dwell with the man;
and the young man was unto him as one of his sons. And
Micah consecrated the Levite; and the young man became
his priest, and was in the house of Micah" (vv. 11, 12). The
proud owner of the temple escorted him around the building, and his eyes shone with satisfaction as he entrusted
the care of the shrine to the young priest from Bethlehem.
The newcomer turned away, and was content. This was
vastly different from the other sanctuary in which he had

served. It would appear that he had been demoted; but had he? "Ten shekels of silver by the year, and a suit of apparel, and thy food" (v. 10). Demotion or promotion? It all depended upon one's viewpoint. Why did this priest accept the position? (i) *If he had sinned,* was this the continuation of his rebellion? Did he rejoice at the possibility of carrying his enmity a little further? (ii) *If he had been ambitious,* did the new offer appear to be the chance of a lifetime? He could become a high priest in his own right, and his financial embarrassment would disappear for ever. (iii) *If he had been restless,* had his journey produced loneliness? Did he enter the employ of Micah in order to find fellowship? Arrayed in new vestments he ministered in Micah's temple, but behold, *an angel in rags!*

An Unholy Priest—Why?

When the Danites came to steal the cherished idols (18:11-26) they said to the priest, "Hold thy peace, lay thy hand upon thy mouth, and go with us, and be to us a father and a priest: is it better for thee to be a priest unto the house of one man, or that thou be a priest unto a tribe and a family in Israel? And the priest's heart was glad, and he took the ephod, and the teraphim, and the graven image, and went in the midst of the people." It was not difficult to break the commandment "Thou shalt not steal," for he had already broken the greatest commandment, "Thou shalt have no other gods before Me." And in new surroundings, the house of idols became the greatest treasure of the Danites—*And all the time the house of God was in Shiloh* (18:31). All the ambitions of the Levite had been realized. He was a great man, and had probably become wealthy. He could laugh at the silent impotence of the place in Shiloh, for he had prospered amazingly since the time when he threw off the restraint of that irksome sanctuary. He had demonstrated the fact that a man could get along quite nicely without God and His house. Yes, his heart was filled with satisfaction—and then, alas, it was time to die. Suddenly his idols seemed to be unresponsive, and his desperate prayers remained unanswered. And then he was summoned to stand before God. He was pale and speechless; he was bankrupt. He had gained a world but had lost his soul.

THE BENJAMITES . . . who found sanctuary in a cave

(JUDGES 20:44-47)

It was horrible; it was disgustingly revolting, and the conscience of the nation was up in arms. Crowds thronged the market places of the cities, for there in full view of the public was a piece of flesh—human flesh. Again and again the story was told, and the constant reiteration only added to the gruesome details. The Benjamites had transgressed; they had committed an unpardonable sin; they had forfeited the right to be known as children of God. They should die! "Then all the children of Israel went out, and the congregation was gathered together as one man, from Dan even to Beersheba, with the land of Gilead, unto the Lord in Mizpeh . . . four hundred thousand footmen that drew sword" (Judges 20:1, 2). They meant business.

The Great Sin

And all the while, a silent sombre man remembered the tragic night when his concubine had been ruthlessly dragged away into the darkness. Flaming passions, unrestrained evil had claimed a defenceless victim, and all through a night of terror, hell's fury had fallen on a poor woman. At dawn they left her broken in body and soul, and alone, upon hands and knees, she wearily crawled homeward. She had been a great sinner, but mercy cried aloud as that pitiable object struggled along the street. "And her lord rose up in the morning, and opened the door of the house, and went out to go his way: and, behold, the woman his concubine was fallen down at the door of the house, and her hands were upon the threshold. And he said unto her, Up, and let us be going. But none answered. Then the man took her up upon an ass . . . and gat him unto his place . . . and he took a knife . . . and divided her . . . and sent her into all the coasts of Israel. And it was so, that all that saw it said, There was no such deed done nor seen from the day that the children of Israel came up out of the land of Egypt unto this day: consider of it, take advice, and speak your minds" (Judges 19:27-30).

33

The Great Danger

A mighty host, the avenging army went forth to battle, and civil war came to the land. The remaining Benjamites refused to deliver the guilty men, and rallying all their fighting strength, they prepared to resist the invaders. Their lips curled in insolent arrogance—they would teach their interfering cousins to mind their own business! The battle proceeded, and slowly righteousness triumphed. Lured from their stronghold to pursue an apparently beaten enemy, the defenders suddenly discovered that they were caught between two armies, and as their men were mown down, the realization of impending disaster gripped every survivor. They were in deadly danger. Eighteen thousand Benjamites lay dead or dying on that gruesome battlefield, and unless some respite could be gained, every defender would be slain. "And they turned and fled toward the wilderness unto the rock Rimmon" (v. 45), but even as they ran, their relentless adversaries attacked on the flanks, and another seven thousand despairing men went down fighting.

The Great Refuge

When someone shouted, "The rock Rimmon," it seemed like a message from heaven; and instantly the remaining men fled for their lives to nature's stronghold. The great cave was so fashioned that it could be held against a multitude. It was very spacious and very safe, so " . . . six hundred men turned and fled to . . . the rock Rimmon, and abode in the rock Rimmon four months" (v. 47). And only thus was the guilty tribe saved from complete annihilation. How great their sin! How great their shelter! How great their safety! They escaped death by inches—a death they had richly deserved. We wonder if the New Testament writer had this scene in mind when he wrote his enchanting text in Hebrews 6:18, "We . . . who have fled for refuge." Perhaps the hymnist was also acquainted with our story when he wrote—

> Oh, safe to the Rock that is higher than I,
>   My soul in its conflicts and sorrows would fly;
> So sinful, so weary, Thine, Thine would I be;
>   Thou blest Rock of Ages, I'm hiding in Thee.

However much we deplore the hatefulness of the Benjamite story, the final details will beget a warm response in our souls. Spiritual need always leads a man to Christ.

NAOMI AND RUTH . . . who came home to Bethlehem

They stood together on the road, two lonely, determined women, whose hearts had been united by the common bond of sorrow. Far back across the years, Naomi still saw the failing crops, the prolonged droughts, and the distressing seasons which had suggested the removal of her family from Bethlehem. Her husband, Elimelech, had been driven almost to the point of despair, and had been fully convinced that Moab alone offered relief from the famine which threatened the home. The little family had moved to the new land, only to discover that hardship knew no frontiers. Her husband and her two sons had died before the resolve to return home had triumphed. Orpah, the other daughter-in-law, had been persuaded to rejoin her people; but Ruth had steadfastly refused to follow her example. In reply to Naomi's suggestion, she answered, " Intreat me not to leave thee . . . thy people shall be my people, and thy God my God. Where thou diest, will I die, and there will I be buried: the Lord do so to me, and more also, if ought but death part thee and me " (Ruth 1:16, 17). And so, hand in hand, they came home to Bethlehem.

The World Needs to Walk that Pathway in Order to Find Peace

It is worthy of note that these two women were very different. Racially and religiously, they once had nothing in common. Naomi was a Jewess, steeped in the traditions of her people; Ruth was a Gentile, a maiden of Moab, and one of a people who were classed as Israel's enemies. The power of love had overcome their scruples, and any feelings of animosity had been banished by their mutual affection. They were no longer Jew and Gentile—they were mother and daughter, united in sorrow, in fellowship, and in the common purpose to allow nothing to separate them. And so they came to Bethlehem. The world needs to follow their sublime example. When Jew and Gentile, European and Asiatic, East and West, can forget their differences and join hands in friendship and love; when all can tread the path to the holy place, then the problems of a world will be solved.

The Backslider Needs to Walk That Pathway in Order to find Peace

Bethlehem was known as " the place of bread," but God had permitted famine to threaten the securities of the district, and alas, one family at least had been unequal to the time of testing. The prosperity of Moab had appeared to be more desirable than the difficulties of the promised land. So they moved to Moab, where attendance at the sanctuary of God was impossible; where the songs of Zion were seldom heard. Probably they made money, for they felt equal to the task of supporting two daughters-in-law; yet disaster overtook them. This story seems to be very modern. Every backslider journeys to Moab, where the famine is of another type, and where the grave-diggers are always busy. Wise men realize that a loaf of bread in Bethlehem is far more satisfying than a sumptuous repast in Moab.

The Sinner Needs to Walk that Pathway in Order to Find Peace

Naomi had known the fellowship of Bethlehem, but Ruth was a complete stranger to its charms. Naomi was a child of Israel, Ruth was a child of heathenism. Probably some lessons concerning the true God had been taught her by her mother-in-law. The daughter's admiring eyes had recognised fortitude in sorrow, and had come to appreciate that divine help was a reality in the experience of her lonely relative. Happy indeed must be every Naomi who can attract others to her God. When Ruth exclaimed, " Thy God shall be my God," her testimony provided the greatest compliment ever paid to the value of Naomi's influence. Naomi had won a convert, and " they two went until they came to Bethlehem." Soon everything came right, for God worked on their behalf in an amazing fashion. Wedding bells filled their souls with gladness, and the laughing eyes of a baby boy removed all sorrow from their hearts. And probably even God smiled, for in the fullness of time Ruth became the great-grandmother of David (Ruth 4:21-22).

KING SAUL . . . who threw away his crown

The riches of grace are not exhausted by regeneration, and this fact is clearly set forth in Paul's letter to the Romans. Chapters 1-4 speak of God's Gospel for the sinner; chapters 5-8, of God's Gospel for the saint. Paul mentions two things. (i) Reconciliation through Christ, enabling us *to enter into life;* (ii) Abundance of grace, enabling us *to reign in life.* Citizenship and kingship are not the same.

The Place of Kingship

Saul had been taken from the plough to become the king of Israel, but even his best friends were beginning to question his suitability for the great position. He had been *called, chosen, crowned,* and presented with unrivalled opportunities. He was God's man, and might have emancipated and exalted the nation to heights of unprecedented splendour. Alas, his increasing arrogance and stupidity led to disaster, and even the prophet Samuel was gravely concerned with the spiritual behaviour of his protégé. Then things suddenly moved toward a climax. " Samuel also said unto Saul, The Lord sent me to anoint thee to be king over his people, over Israel: now therefore hearken thou . . . Go and smite Amalek, and utterly destroy all that they have, and spare them not; but slay both man and woman, infant and suckling, ox and sheep, camel and ass " (I Sam. 15:1-3). Kingship demands great qualifications.

The Price of Kingship

The commission included three great clauses. (i) *No cowardice.* The enemies had to be engaged in battle, and ruthlessly exterminated. Their moral and spiritual decadence could be tolerated no longer. (ii) *No compromise.* The tempting possessions of the condemned nation had to be renounced, and the sin of Achan avoided. (iii) *No condemnation.* If Saul faithfully observed the commandments of the Lord, divine favour would immeasurably enrich his kingdom. If he failed, his kingship would be imperilled. The New Testament also emphasizes this truth. Union with Christ in the heavenly places means unceasing warfare against evil. Compromise on the spiritual battlefields leads to defeat; sacrificial self-denial is the price of power.

The Peril of Kingship

" And Saul smote the Amalekites . . . and he took Agag the king . . . alive, and utterly destroyed all the people with the edge of the sword. But Saul and the people spared Agag, and the best of the sheep, and of the oxen, and of the fatlings, and the lambs, and all that was good, and would not utterly destroy them: but everything that was vile and refuse, that they destroyed utterly " (vv. 7-9). Saul spared the condemned beasts because he coveted them; and Agag was permitted to live because it pleased Saul to act benevolently. And in this way he demonstrated his unfitness for high office. " Samuel came to Saul: and Saul said unto him, Blessed be thou of the Lord: I have performed the commandment of the Lord. And Samuel said, what meaneth then this bleating of the sheep in mine ears, and the lowing of the oxen which I hear? And Saul said, *They* have brought them . . . to sacrifice unto the Lord . . ." (vv. 13-21). Two things seem obvious. (i) He had forgotten that the Lord had already pronounced these offerings to be unclean. No man should offer anything but the best to God. (ii) If he offered other people's animals, he could retain his own. Selfishness overshadowed all his service.

The Power of Kingship

Thus God rejected Saul from being King over Israel, and the deposed monarch was never so despicable as when he blamed his people. " I have obeyed . . . but the people took of the spoil " (vv. 20, 21). Therefore the privilege of ruling Israel was given to David, for none can occupy a position of supreme importance in the kingdom of God unless he is conformed to the divine will. The boy from Bethlehem satisfied the requirements of the Almighty, and became God's instrument of blessing to the nation. Poor Saul! His story teaches that if we would be enthroned in heavenly places (Ephes. 2:1-4) we must be crucified with Christ. Then self will be silent when we go forth to fight the battles of the Lord.

ABIATHAR . . . the sole survivor from a massacred city

Such a thing had never been known in Israel. King
Saul had murdered a city of priests, and had thereby
sealed his doom. He had heard how they had helped
David, and, frustrated by his own inability to capture the
young prince, he was furious. He snarled, and demanded
adequate reasons why the clerics should help the enemy
of the throne. "Then Ahimelech answered the king, and
said, And who is so faithful among all thy servants as
David, which is the king's son-in-law, and goeth at thy
bidding, and is honourable in thine house?" (1 Sam.
22:14). The calm, dignified answer annoyed Saul, and he
fiercely replied, "Thou shalt surely die, Ahimelech, thou,
and all thy father's house. And the king said unto the
footmen that stood about him, Turn and slay the priests
of the Lord. But the servants of the king would not . . .
And the king said to Doeg, Turn thou and fall upon the
priests. And Doeg the Edomite . . . fell upon the priests,
and slew on that day fourscore and five persons that did
wear a linen ephod. And Nob, the city of the priests,
smote he with the edge of the sword" (vv. 16-19). And
the watching madman—for mad Saul must have been—
could not see that his actions would become the greatest
boomerang in history.

A Great Distress

"And one of the sons of Ahimelech the son of Ahitub,
named Abiathar, escaped, and fled after David" (v. 20).
We do not know how the boy managed to evade the
cruel sword of the Edomite. Possibly in the confusion
he was able to dodge away through the ranks of sullen
footmen. The soldiers were angry but impotent as their
royal leader pronounced the despicable death sentence,
and risked their lives when they refused to obey a command. It is not too much to suppose, therefore, that if
opportunity arose they gladly assisted the fleeing boy.
Abiathar ran for his life, and when he was able to rest for
a few moments he realized that he was alone in the world,
and friendless. Storm clouds filled his sky, and Saul
seemed likely to hound him to death. Then he remem-

bered the fugitive prince. Yes, he would go to David and ask for help.

A Great Decision

Slowly, carefully, the young man made his way toward the cave of Adullam. He quickly found the hillside trail, and commenced the ascent; but almost immediately a rough voice commanded him to stand still. Startled, he obeyed, and a toughened sentry stepped from a hiding place to ask the cause of this intrusion. " Young man, where are you going, and why?" The boy told his story, and confessed he wished to reach David. The older man's eyes were filled with sympathy as he saw the boy's grief, and if Abiathar asked, " Do you think David will take me in? " the sentry hastened to dispel his fears. " Son, of course he will. He is the friend of all the needy. My boy, didn't you hear that ' every one that was in distress, and every one that was in debt, and every one that was bitter of soul, gathered themselves unto him; and he became a captain over them: and there were with him about four hundred men '? (I Sam. 22:2). Son, I came to him, and I found a welcome. What he did for me, he will do for you. Go ahead. All is well."

A Great Deliverance

" And Abiathar shewed David that Saul had slain the Lord's priests. And David said unto Abiathar . . . Abide thou with me, fear not : for he that seeketh my life seeketh thy life : but with me thou shalt be in safeguard " (1 Sam. 22:21-23). That day the young man discovered three wonderful facts. (i) *A place to rest.* His own home had been destroyed, and the old surroundings were now prohibited to him. The birds had their nests, but he had no place to call *home* until he bowed before a charming prince who welcomed him into the fellowship of a new society. " My boy, stay here and rest." (ii) *A promise to reassure.* " Fear not . . . with me thou shalt be in safeguard." Abide with me. I will be your protection; my words shall be your delight; my men shall be your brothers; and my presence shall be your home. (iii) *A peace to enjoy.* Abiathar looked into the face of his new friend, and a new calm settled upon his tired spirit, and he lay down to rest.

THE WITCH OF ENDOR . . . and her cry in the night

The house was eerie and still, as the witch awaited the arrival of her visitors. She was unhappy and uncertain; her life was in danger. People had heard that she dabbled in the unknown, and the fact that a mysterious personage had sought her help filled her with fear. She listened intently for the sounds of footsteps. She had been assured that this was no trap, and her clients had appeared to be men of honour. The times were hard, or she would have resisted this temptation to earn money. Suddenly she heard people stealthily approaching her door, and her lips quivered. They were coming! It was to be hoped they had preserved the secret of their mission.

A Witch in Danger

Her art was unpopular and unlawful in Israel. Each time the reigning monarch rededicated his life to God, his zeal was manifested in a new witch-hunt. The law of Moses condemned spiritist mediums, and necromancers were obliged to flee from the hands of justice. The divine commandment had been clearly given: "There shall not be found among you any one that maketh his son or his daughter to pass through the fire, or that useth divination, or an observer of times, or an enchanter, or a witch, or a charmer, or a consulter with familiar spirits, or *a necromancer* (one who seeks to commune with the dead). For all that do these things are an abomination unto the Lord" (Deut. 18:10-12). "And the soul that turneth after such . . . I will even set my face against that soul, and will cut him off from among his people" (Lev. 20:6). "A man also or a woman that hath a familiar spirit, or that is a wizard, shall surely be put to death: they shall stone them with stones: their blood shall be on them" (Lev. 20:27). No spiritist medium was safe when Israel turned to God.

A Witch in Demand

"And when Saul enquired of the Lord, the Lord answered him not, neither by dreams, nor by Urim, nor by prophets. Then Saul said unto his servants, Seek me a woman that hath a familiar spirit, that I may go to her, and enquire of her. And his servants said to him, Behold there is a woman that hath a familiar spirit at Endor" (1 Sam. 28: 6-7). Saul's sin had raised a barrier between his soul and God. True repentance would have removed that hindrance, but the fear which filled the king's heart was not repentance. That the witch-hunter could seek the co-operation of a condemned woman seems to testify that God was not indispensable. He would seek elsewhere what the Lord would not give. Disguised, he came to the witch and asked her to bring up Samuel. It may be true that a great deal of psychic phenomena has been placed at the disposal of men, but nothing can alter the fact that the word of the Highest repeatedly denounces the practice of seeking to communicate with the dead. Every Christian will know that the saints are " absent from the body and at home with the Lord."

A Witch in Distress

It is most remarkable that the witch was undismayed when Saul asked her to bring up Samuel. Calmly, she received the request, and there is no doubt that had she been given a little time, she would have proceeded with her usual incantations. However, the sudden, unannounced appearance of the prophet took her completely by surprise, and her loud startled cry echoed through the house. Obviously she had nothing to do with the return of the prophet, and was most unhappy in his presence. " She cried with a loud voice " (v. 12). If any further denunciation of the practice of spiritism were necessary, it would be supplied by Samuel's message to Saul. The man of God spoke of divine wrath, the hatefulness of sin, and the emptiness of a life from which God withdraws Himself. Do spiritist mediums deliver messages of that calibre? Does any messenger from the other world turn a séance into an evangelistic meeting where men and women are reminded of the necessity to repent of sin and turn to God? " So Saul died for his transgression which he committed against the Lord, even against the word of the Lord, which he kept not, *and also for asking counsel of one that had a familiar spirit,* to enquire of it " (1 Chron. 10: 13). It is far better to seek the guidance of a prophet while he is still alive, than to wait until he is dead. Be in time!

THE WOMAN OF TEKOAH . . . Israel's
famous actress
(2 SAMUEL 14:1-23)

" Now Joab the son of Zeruiah perceived that the king's heart was toward Absalom," and the matter caused grave concern. Joab sighed as he remembered the tragic events of former years. Absalom's favourite sister had been seduced by her evil step-brother, and the proud prince had ruthlessly planned to exterminate Amnon. His schemes had succeeded, and fleeing before justice, Absalom had gone to a distant land. All these details were well known throughout the nation; but Joab, the most intimate of the king's friends, knew that David was grieving. " And Joab sent to Tekoah, and fetched thence a wise woman, and said unto her, I pray thee, feign thyself to be a mourner, and put on mourning apparel, and anoint not thyself with oil, but be as a woman that had a long time mourned for the dead. And come to the king and speak on this manner unto him. So Joab put the words in her mouth " (2 Sam. 14:2, 3).

Her Great Sorrow

She was a great actress. Only those with similar gifts will understand how she succeeded in deceiving her royal master, for as king David listened to her pitiful cry, his heart melted. " What aileth thee? " he asked; and she replied, " I am indeed a widow woman, and mine husband is dead " (vv. 4, 5). Then she told the heart-rending account of her two boys fighting in the field, and how one had been slain. She described how the rest of her family now demanded the slayer's execution, and how she was in danger of losing her second boy. Her body shook with suppressed sobbing as she unfolded her sad story. When she lifted a tear-stained face to look at king David, he saw her anguish, and said, " Go to thine house, and I will give charge concerning thee " (v. 8). Still she continued until the king, irritated by her persistence, exclaimed, " As the Lord liveth, there shall not one hair of thy son fall to the earth " (v. 11). Then as he watched, a transformation took place before him, and he became speechless with wonder.

Her Great Sermon

Slowly she shook the dust from her dress; she threw back her cloak, and immediately David perceived a change in her demeanour. Her eyes filled with accusations as she said, " The king doth speak this thing as one that is faulty, in that the king doth not fetch home again his banished " (v. 13). King David, you swear that my boy shall be protected. Why, then, do you not protect your own son who occupies a similar position? " For we must needs die, and are as water spilt on the ground . . . neither doth God respect any person: *yet doth he devise means that his banished be not expelled from him "* (v. 14). King David, you believe in the law and the prophets; you regularly offer the sacrifices. Why is this so? Is it not because God has made provision whereby His sinful children may draw near to His footstool? Although through the folly of sin we may be banished from His presence, God's grace does not expel us for ever. We may bring our offerings and confess our sins, and at the altar of mercy receive pardon. If God can do such things, should you not follow His example?

Her Great Success

Against the wiles of this talented actress, David had no defence. Ultimately he asked, " Is not the hand of Joab with thee in all this? " (v. 19). Then the king was told the complete story, and finally he sent for his trusted servant and said, " Behold now, I have done this thing: go therefore, bring the young man Absalom again " (v. 21). The actress bowed in the dust, and her eyes were smiling. She had played to the smallest audience of her career, but this had been her greatest performance. In spite of the fact that her theological outlook was limited to a Tabernacle, the laws of Moses, and the daily offerings, she presented an outstanding case before the royal judge, and won the verdict. We can only imagine what she might have said had she been able to speak of the love of God in Christ; the reconciliation made through the cross, and the glorious Gospel of saving grace. In very deed and truth, " he doth devise means that his banished be not expelled from him." Dear lady, we salute you! What a pity you are unable to stand in our pulpits. Our churches would be packed to capacity if you were the preacher.

AHITHOPHEL . . . the man who could not forgive

(2 SAMUEL 17:23)

The cause of God is always greater than the man who represents it, and no one can ever be justified in leaving his place of service because he has discovered sin in high places of responsibility. Ahithophel was one of the greatest men of his time, but he allowed memories of injustice to colour his entire horizon.

Ahithophel's Greatness

This eminent man occupied one of the stately homes of Israel, for he was not only a great man in his own right, he was the bosom friend and honoured counsellor of the king. When he gave counsel " he spake as the oracle of God," and on innumerable occasions the king had cause to thank God for the presence of his old and trusted friend. Now, Ahithophel had a son whose name was Eliam (2 Sam. 23:34), a distinguished captain in David's army. He was very proud of his boy, and perhaps even more proud of his beautiful grandchild Bath-sheba (2 Sam. 11:3). He watched her and wistfully thought of the future, and when Uriah the Hittite, another valiant captain, fell in love with this charming girl, both her father and grandfather joyously consented to their marriage. And then came tragedy!

Ahithophel's Grief

" And it came to pass in an eveningtide, that David arose from off his bed, and walked upon the roof of the king's house: and from the roof he saw a woman washing herself; and the woman was very beautiful to look upon. And David sent and enquired after the woman. And one said, Is not this Bath-sheba, the daughter of Eliam, the wife of Uriah the Hittite? And David sent messengers and took her . . ." (11:2-4). Poor Bath-sheba, she was just a helpless woman in an eastern land—and could hardly be expected to resist the attentions of an irresponsible passionate monarch. The weeks and the months which followed were dark with apprehension and dread. Fearful suspense tortured her mind, and even David regretted the madness of former days. Constantly the threat of discovery hung over his head, and as a last resort he ordered the execution of the faithful young husband. Bath-sheba bowed in sorrow and mourned for her lover, but old grandfather Ahithophel knew no such restraint. This act of David was despicable to the extreme —it was murder! Incensed, the great counsellor saddled his ass and went home to Giloh. Uriah was in the grave; his lovely Bath-sheba had been seduced. The old man was furious.

Ahithophel's Guilt

The subsequent story of David's bitter repentance only hardened Ahithophel's heart. Could tears bring back the dead Uriah? Could tears remove the stain from the soul of a seduced girl? Bah! When Absalom's treachery threatened the safety of King David, Ahithophel heard the news and smiled. Had not David forfeited his right to reign? " And Absalom sent for Ahithophel . . . and the conspiracy was strong. Then said Absalom to Ahithophel, Give counsel among you what we shall do. And Ahithophel said unto Absalom, Go in unto thy father's concubines . . . and all Israel shall hear that thou art abhorred of thy father: then shall the hands of all that are with thee be strong . . . And the counsel of Ahithophel which he counselled in those days was as if a man had enquired at the oracle of God " (2 Sam. 15:12; 16:20-23). Poor man, bitterness had blinded his eyes to the fact that the cause of God is always greater than the man who represents it.

Ahithophel's Grave

The dramatic story of Hushai's opposition to the counsel of Ahithophel, makes good reading. Driven by increasing animosity, David's former friend would have pursued the weary king to slay him. Yet doubt was implanted in Absalom's mind, and ultimately Ahithophel was rejected. " And when Ahithophel saw that his counsel was not followed, he saddled his ass, and arose, and gat him home to his house, to his city, and put his household in order, and hanged himself, and died, and was buried in the sepulchre of his father " (2 Sam. 17:23). Did David ever visit the grave of his old friend? Did he weep as he read the epitaph, " Here lies Ahithophel—the man who could not forgive "?

DAVID . . . who refused a magnificent gift

(2 SAMUEL 24:24)

There was great trouble in Israel; a plague was destroying the people. The king had acted unwisely, and his earnest prayers were seeking forgiveness. " And David said unto the Lord, I have sinned greatly in that I have done: and now, I beseech thee, O Lord, take away the iniquity of thy servant; for I have done very foolishly " (2 Sam. 24:10). His cry of anguish reached the heart of God, and the prophet Gad was sent to reveal a way of escape. " And Gad came that day to David, and said unto him, Go up, rear an altar unto the Lord in the threshingfloor of Araunah the Jebusite. And David went up as the Lord commanded " (vv. 18, 19).

A Present Refused

The farmer was startled when he saw the royal procession coming toward him, and " he bowed himself before the king on his face upon the ground. And Araunah said, Wherefore is my lord the king come to his servant? And David said, To buy the threshingfloor of thee, to build an altar unto the Lord, that the plague may be stayed from the people " (vv. 20, 21). Then the man stood and graciously offered to give everything needed for the carrying out of David's plans. He fully realized that the tide of evil had reached his own property, and soon he and his family would become its victims. " Master," he cried, " You can have it all. I want no money. Take whatsoever you desire and, ' the Lord thy God accept thee '." David's eyes probably became misty as he listened to the words of his subject; yet slowly he shook his head and answered, " Nay; but I will surely buy it of thee at a price: neither will I offer burnt offerings unto the Lord my God of that which doth cost me nothing " (v. 24). Many people are eager to give away other people's possessions; their giving then costs nothing. David refused to belong to this category. He had hurt God; his atonement must hurt him.

A Price Paid

" So David bought the threshingfloor and the oxen for fifty shekels of silver. And David built there an altar unto the Lord" (vv. 24, 25). All true giving to God costs something; and our Lord Jesus Christ provides the greatest example of this fact. He also saw a plague sweeping through a world, and realized that an altar alone could rob it of power. The erection of that altar was not easily accomplished. (i) *He yearned until He wept.* When He saw men as sheep without a shepherd; when He saw a city without hope, nothing could prevent His tears of sorrow. (ii) *He prayed until He bled.* The garden conflict broke His heart, and " his sweat was as it were great drops of blood falling down to the ground." (iii) *He gave until He died.* The triumph of Calvary reveals how great was the price He paid for our salvation. Eternal love was sacrificial love. Is it not a cause for amazement that some who profess His name can offer to their Lord something which costs nothing?

A Plague Removed

" So the Lord was entreated for the land, and the plague was stayed from Israel " (v. 25). And from that day, the people gratefully remembered the threshing-floor of Araunah. The altar and its sacrifice had robbed a plague of power. And Araunah himself had the greatest cause for rejoicing; he might have been dead had not salvation come to his house. Thus even in the twilight ages preceding the coming of Christ, God endeavoured to prepare His people for the glorious Gospel of His salvation. Man's happiness would be eternally linked with an altar, for there the power of sin would be defeated, his own safety be assured, and songs of praise would instinctively arise from his heart. When the news of David's altar spread through the land, suffering people obtained new hope, and it was more than likely that many of them left their homes in search of healing. And if that were the case, they foreshadowed a great host who in the fullness of time sought shelter in the shadow of Calvary's cross.

> I take, O Cross, thy shadow
>   For my abiding place;
> I ask no other sunshine than
>   The sunshine of His face;
> Content to let the world go by,
>   To know no gain nor loss;
> My sinful self my only shame,
>   My glory all the Cross.

48

ELIJAH . . . whose ministry ended in flames

"And Ahab told Jezebel all that Elijah had done, and withal how he had slain all the prophets with the sword. Then Jezebel sent a messenger unto Elijah, saying, So let the gods do to me, and more also, if I make not thy life as the life of one of them by tomorrow about this time. And when Elijah saw that, he arose and went for his life . . . and he came unto a cave, and lodged there . . ." (vv. 1-9). And in that one desperate flight, poor Elijah ruined the work of a lifetime.

A Great Ministry Ruined

Language is inadequate to describe the greatness of the opportunity presented on Mount Carmel. The prophet had suddenly appeared before the nation, and his challenging faith had cornered the opposition. The dramatic intercession of the prophets of Baal had ended in disappointment before Elijah repaired the altar of God and cried to his Creator. The falling fire struck fear into the hearts of the entire congregation, and everyone present had cried, "The Lord, he is the God; the Lord, he is the God" (1 Kings 18:39). The enemies of Israel had been ruthlessly slain, and the way opened for national repentance. The showers of rain confirmed the evidence of the hillside, and everywhere, receptive hearts awaited the leadership of the man so signally honoured by God. True revival was never nearer than it was in those moments: but when victory was within the grasp of God's great man, he threw it away. The threat of Jezebel paralysed his faith, and he fled into obscurity. And for weeks after that sad day, the people talked of his failure, and many of them laughed the prophet to scorn. Poor Elijah!

A Great Mistake Rebuked

"What doest thou here, Elijah?" (19:9). The gentle whisper disturbed the silence of the cave, and the despondent prophet lifted his head. He was not alone! "And he said, I have been very jealous for the Lord God of hosts: for the children of Israel have forsaken thy covenant, thrown down thine altars, and slain thy prophets with the sword; and I, even I only, am left; and they seek my life, to take it away " (v. 10). Poor man! where is the courage that rebuked a nation? Alas, it has gone up in flames! There was no mention of Jezebel, and no reference to his tragic blunder. " And God said, Go forth, and stand upon the mount before the Lord." Elijah witnessed the great manifestations of God in nature, but remained unmoved until he heard the sound of a still small voice. Then he wrapped his head in his mantle and went forth to stand in the mouth of the cave. " And behold, there came a voice unto him, and said, What doest thou here, Elijah? " (v. 13). Are you a preacher? Then what *doest* thou here? Were you called to minister to Israel? Then what doest thou *here*? Are you a prophet of the Highest? Then what doest THOU—HERE? " Yet I have left me seven thousand in Israel, all the knees which have not bowed unto Baal, and every mouth which hath not kissed him "—and you say that you are the only saint left in Israel—Oh, Elijah!

A Great Man Resplendent

The kindness of God is beyond human comprehension. Elijah could never again urge Israel to look to God, and was therefore instructed to call and commission his successor. " So he departed thence, and found Elisha the son of Shaphat, who was ploughing with twelve yoke of oxen before him, and he with the twelfth: and Elijah passed by him, and cast his mantle upon him . . . Then Elisha arose, and went after Elijah and ministered unto him " (vv. 19-21). And these two men were still together when God greatly honoured His prophet. Human failures cannot change the kindness of God. " And it came to pass, as they still went on and talked, that, behold, there appeared a chariot of fire . . . and parted them both asunder; and Elijah went up by a whirlwind into heaven " (2 Kings 2:11). God graciously promoted His servant to higher realms. Instead of ministering *for* the Lord, Elijah had the honour of ministering *to* the Lord. He was sent to the mount of transfiguration to commune with the Lord Jesus.

> Grace, grace: God's grace;
> Grace that can pardon and cleanse within.
> Grace, grace: God's grace:
> Grace that is greater than all our sin.

NAAMAN . . . who lost a great opportunity

(2 KINGS 5:18)

Dear Naaman,

I have often wanted to speak with you, for your amazing story has caused a great amount of discussion. You will probably be pleased to know that millions of people are grateful that your history has been placed on record. I, for example, first heard of you when I was a small boy. My Sunday-school teacher told me how you went to battle and brought away captive out of the land of Israel, a little maid. I sometimes felt sorry for that girl, but eventually the greatness of your story captivated all my thought. I saw you marching to the palace of the king of Israel, and I laughed at the tantrums of the outraged monarch who thought the whole thing was a plot against his régime. Yes, Naaman, my childhood days were coloured by stories of great heroes, and you were one of the greatest. And then, I discovered something about you that spoiled everything.

Your Great Salvation

You were very angry, weren't you, when the prophet failed to make a fuss of you. Because you were a great man in your country, you thought the prophet of God should have been honoured by your visit. You did not know that all who come to God must possess the humility of children. Were you very surprised when your servant suggested that your wrath revealed folly? And were you a little ashamed when obedience to the prophet's command brought healing to your body? I imagined your going down into the water, and the subsequent return to the home of Elisha. Surely even the angels smiled when they saw the change in your attitude. Your testimony really thrilled me. " Behold, now I know that there is no God in all the earth, but in Israel . . ." (2 Kings 5:15). Yes, your conversion was outstanding, and preachers have used this story on innumerable occasions. They tell their audiences that in like manner men may be cleansed from the leprosy of sin; that what the waters of Jordan apparently did for you, the precious blood of Christ will do for all who will " wash and be clean."

Your Great Suggestion

Naaman, what a grand idea you had when you stood before the prophet. " Shall there not then, I pray thee, be given to thy servant two mules' burden of earth? for thy servant will henceforth offer neither burnt offering nor sacrifice unto other gods, but unto the Lord " (v. 17). In thought I watched as you filled the sacks with earth, and I visualized the small altar which you made in your own land. Yes, your idea was very fine, and suited your earlier confession. Henceforth God alone would receive the thankofferings of your heart. He had become the God of your salvation, and was worthy to be praised. That soil was holy ground, where you often knelt as you drew near to God. For that we commend you heartily; but oh, dear friend, why did you ruin everything? Naaman, you were a mean coward!

Your Great Silence

Do you refute the allegation? Listen, then, to your own words. " In this thing the Lord pardon thy servant, that when my master goeth into the house of Rimmon to worship there, and he leaneth on my hand, *and I bow myself in the house of Rimmon,* the Lord pardon thy servant in this thing " (v. 18). Didn't you realize that all Syria awaited your return? Didn't you realize that the great God had placed within your grasp the most magnificent opportunity? Your fellows were heathen, and had no knowledge of God, and your testimony might have been instrumental in evangelizing a nation. Had you refused to bow before Rimmon, and had you become a prophet to your own people, thousands of Syrians might have called you " blessed." Instead, when the thanksgiving service was held in the temple; when the king returned thanks to his idol, all the people gathered there, watched as you followed his example. Oh, Naaman, why were you ashamed to own your Lord? Were you fearful of losing your position of importance and rank? Were you scared lest another should supersede you in the affections of a heathen king? Naaman, you revealed in the cause of God a cowardice unknown in your military career. You let God down. What a pity!

JEHU . . . and the famous handshake

(2 KINGS 10:15)

The story of how the ancient Order of the Rechabites came into being is one of great interest. The founder was Rechab, the father of Jehonadab; and the earliest meetings of the noble society took place in a simple Hebrew home. From time to time, this grand old man gathered his family together and instructed them in the ways of happiness. War had ravaged the nation, and the taverns were filled with drinking men. It was during these troubled days that Rechab commenced his " Band of Hope." Jehonadab, his son, was an apt pupil, and in later years continued the father's work (Jer. 35:5-6).

The Charm of a Gracious Man

It is a great mistake to imagine that all people outside the Christian Church are villains and reprobates. That all have sinned and come short of the glory of God, there can be no doubt; but there are innumerable people whose early home influence has had a remarkable effect in the building of character. Such an one was the young ruler who could justly claim that he had kept the commandments from infancy. *True* greatness of soul, however, does not lead to self-sufficiency: rather, it begets unqualified admiration for all that is gentle, gracious, and good. True virtue will be attracted to Absolute Goodness, and will never be repelled by Him in whom such standards were manifest. The fragrance of Jehonadab's life was well known in Israel, and when he heard of Jehu's activities on behalf of God, his soul was thrilled. "And when Jehu was departed thence, he lighted on Jehonadab the son of Rechab *coming to meet him* " (2 Kings 10:15).

The Challenge of a Glorious Master

The story of the anointing of Jehu makes exciting reading (2 Kings 9:1-6). The unparalleled enthusiasm with which he performed his duties electrified Israel, for a glorious abandon was revealed in all his actions. The news that God had visited His people spread from Dan to Beersheba, and all men talked of the new leader. Yet the heart of Jehu was inclined toward Jehonadab, and eventually he set forth in search of him. Jehonadab saw the chariot rushing toward him, and stepped aside to watch as the driver calmed and halted the plunging horses. Admiration shone in his eyes when he recognized superb horsemanship. Beneath the touch of this amazing man, the beasts were either docile or infuriated. There was no need for an introduction, as both realized each other's identity. Then Jehu said, " Is thine heart right, as my heart is with thine heart? "—Young man, I have heard of you, and I admit that my heart has responded to that which I have heard. Young man, I am greatly attracted to you, but are you attracted to me? " Is thy heart right with mine, as my heart is with thine? And Jehonadab answered, It is." The ancient scene is very attractive. Jehu had realized that such a man would be an asset in the great cause, and it had become a matter of primary importance that Jehonadab should be challenged with a new call. And this is in keeping with all God's dealings with man. True goodness will attract the Lord Jesus, just as Jehonadab attracted Jehu.

The Claims of a Great Ministry

Jehu looked into the shining eyes of his young friend, and smiled as he heard the answer. Then suddenly he stretched forth his hand and said, " If it be, give me thine hand. And Jehonadab gave him his hand, and Jehu took him up to him into the chariot." Holy passions transfigured Jehu's face as he cried, " Come with me, and see my zeal for the Lord." And through all the subsequent story Jehonadab was at the side of the great reformer as he endeavoured to rid Israel of the idolatry which had been her curse. Together these great men worked for the salvation of the nation. Jehonadab's affection was ceaselessly expressed in his wholehearted service. He not only had faith in the great cause; he served it. To him, and to his master Jehu, " faith without works " would have been dead. It was at this point that the rich young ruler failed the Lord Jesus. He, too, had faith, and an intense desire to possess eternal life. Yet when the claims of Christ's ministry made demands upon his possessions, talents, and time, he turned away. Jehonadab had greater wisdom, for his best was placed at the feet of his Lord. He placed his hand into the hand of his leader, and left it there. We shall be wise to follow his example.

HULDAH . . . the prophetess who pressed suits

(2 KINGS 22:14)

A certain famous clothing firm has specialized in the advertisement, " You can always tell a man by the way he is dressed," and a little while ago the appearance of their sandwich-board man in the streets of Glasgow caused a great deal of mirth. He patiently walked up and down the main streets proclaiming to all and sundry the virtue of being dressed by his employers—yet he himself was a tramp in rags. Huldah the prophetess was probably a very handy woman to have in the royal palace. Her constant care of the royal wardrobe assured the king that his various uniforms were always ready for use. Every Christian has been presented with a similar wardrobe, and this demands constant attention. Huldah should be the example of every follower of Christ.

The Garment of Salvation

" I will greatly rejoice in the Lord . . . for he hath clothed me with the garments of salvation, he hath covered me with a robe of righteousness " (Isa. 61:10). After their act of disobedience, Adam and Eve patiently made garments with which to clothe themselves; and as far as we are able to judge, they were very satisfied with their efforts. Yet when the voice of God sounded in the garden, they fled; for they realized that in spite of their commendable efforts, they were still naked. The demoniac of Gadara furiously tore the clothing from his body, for in his unbalanced state of mind, he considered his appearance to be perfectly satisfactory. Yet when Christ expelled the indwelling demons, the man realised his great need and gladly accepted the garment which Christ offered. The most elementary Gospel truth teaches that man's best righteousness is as filthy rags; that he is naked in the sight of the Lord, and needs to be clothed with the garment of salvation.

The Garment of Holiness

". . and the holy garments for Aaron the priest, and the garments of his sons, to minister in the priest's office " (Ex. 31:10). Divine law required that he who entered within the veil to intercede on behalf of Israel, should be clothed in consecrated vestments. He who would prevail in the secret place should be suitably arrayed to reveal the magnificence of his office. Thus we are introduced to the next item of the royal wardrobe. He who claims allegiance to Christ and professes His salvation, should be clothed in the garment of holiness; for there is no one so disappointing as the man who fails to practise what he preaches. If Christ be the object of my admiration, it logically follows that His holiness will be my example.

The Garment of Humility

". . . be clothed with humility: for God resisteth the proud, and giveth grace to the humble " (1 Pet. 5:5). That the apostle Peter should give this advice to the elders of the Church seems to suggest that if *they* needed to be humble, then the entire assembly needed the same grace. Holiness and humility are twin sisters. They belong to each other. There are people who advertise their holiness and at the same time strut about like peacocks. There are truly godly saints who proclaim to all and sundry, " I am the chief of sinners." Humility is the shy emanation of inward godliness; spiritual pride is the evidence that one's head has outgrown one's heart; that one's holiness is but a reflection of self-esteem.

The Garment of Praise

". . . the garment of praise for the spirit of heaviness." This suggestive portion of Isaiah's prophecy was read by the Saviour in the synagogue at Nazareth (Luke 4:16-22); and when He went on to say, " This day is the Scripture fulfilled in your ears," He clearly demonstrated that He had come to give joy. One cannot walk with Christ and remain sad, for the very essence of His message leads to joy. At the conclusion of His ministry He said " These things have I spoken unto you, that *your joy might be full.*" The Christian wardrobe contains a glorious selection of exquisite clothing; but this adds to our responsibility. Huldah's activities seem to say, " You can always tell a man by the way he is dressed."

THE QUEEN OF SHEBA . . . who argued
herself into a journey (2 CHRONICLES 9:1-12)

The queen of Sheba was one of the most glamorous figures in the ancient world. The fame of this illustrious woman had spread to many countries, for the splendour of her court was both lavish and sensational. Amid a magnificence peculiarly her own, this attractive lady reigned supreme, and it was difficult to believe that any other kingdom could be more brilliant than hers. When itinerant merchants spoke of the surpassing splendour of Israel, and described the amazing wisdom of king Solomon, her eyes speculatively narrowed; and then, smiling, she dismissed the accounts as the exaggerations of overworked imaginations. Many years later, the Lord Jesus introduced this eminent woman into the Gospel story, and in the light of that introduction it is now possible to advance three propositions—

The Wonder of the Gospel is almost beyond comprehension

To say the least, nothing like this had hitherto been known. David's kingdom had been great, but the messengers claimed superlative splendour for Solomon. Could not these men be guilty of speaking untruthfully? Yet each time she examined their wares, and handled their treasures, she saw evidence in support of their claim. How could they possess such gems, and offer such goods, if their supplies were not obtained in a land of plenty? Her mind was greatly disturbed as she considered these possibilities. In like manner the story of the Gospel speaks to us of the greatness of the Kingdom of Christ. We are told of the gold of grace; the pearls of pardon; and the rich jewels of redeeming love, so plentiful in the realm of the spirit. The wonder of the Gospel message beggars description; yet every thinking man becomes confused when he recognises a true Christian. The radiance of a consecrated life suggests that such jewels surely come from a Kingdom of plenty.

The Challenge of the Gospel is almost beyond dispute

The palace of the queen of Sheba became a centre of animated debate, as each new merchant repeated his claim. Ultimately the challenge of the message overcame the unbelief of the woman, and she prepared to confirm or disprove the story for ever. That the message could be so tested was to her a great source of satisfaction. And thus the historian wrote, "And when the queen of Sheba heard of the fame of Solomon, she came to prove Solomon with hard questions at Jerusalem . . . and when she was come to Solomon, she communed with him of all that was in her heart" (2 Chron. 9:1). In her search for evidence, she obtained thrilling results. The present-day world has also become a debating centre, and various findings have been released for the edifying of communities. Yet the greatest challenge has been ignored. If men came to Christ to test the claims of the Gospel, they would soon say, "Behold, the one half of the greatness of thy wisdom was not told me: for thou exceedest the fame that I heard. Happy are thy men, and happy are these thy servants . . ." (vv. 6, 7).

The Sufficiency of the Gospel is almost beyond description

"And king Solomon gave to the queen of Sheba all her desire, *whatsoever she asked,* beside that which Solomon gave her of his royal bounty. So she turned and went to her own country, she and her servants" (1 Kings 10:13). Prayer is the key which unlocks heaven's treasure house. The enrichment of the ancient queen is a suggestive picture of the untold treasures obtainable at the throne of grace. Emulating the example of the royal lady, we bring our gifts to Christ, and He says, "Ask what ye will, and it shall be done." She was not impoverished by her giving to Solomon; and neither are we when we give to Christ. Our thankofferings are returned "shaken together, pressed down, and running over." And from the day of her return to Sheba's palace, the queen joyfully anticipated the coming of the merchants. Her debating ceased, as her home became a place of testimony. She had seen the great king, and loved to hear news of his kingdom. We are grateful to the ancient lady for supplying the world with such a colourful picture of God's saving grace. She was a wise woman who went in search of reality, and found it! And Jesus said, "The queen of the south shall rise up in the judgment with the men of this generation, and shall condemn it: for she came from the uttermost parts of the earth to hear the wisdom of Solomon; and, behold, a greater than Solomon is here" (Matt. 12:42).

JEHOSHAPHAT . . . the king who sank his navy

(2 Chronicles 20:35-37)

Unholy alliances between saint and sinner were never in the will of God, and Christians who enter into such partnership cannot expect to receive the blessing of the Almighty. This applies to business, matrimony, and any other realm where temptation seeks to undermine the righteous. Against the sombre background of history, the command of God is clearly written: "Be not unequally yoked together with unbelievers" (2 Cor. 6:14). It is an indisputable fact that most of the people who have made shipwreck of their Christian testimony have done so because they failed to observe this important command. History is filled with examples of this type; but one of the most startling is that of Jehoshaphat, whose madness sent a fleet of great vessels to the bottom of the sea.

A Great Faith Singing

The silly monarch who entered into a fatal alliance with evil should have known better! Previous experience had taught him the value of obedience to the will of God; and for the tragedy which eventually overwhelmed him, he had no one to blame but himself. Years before he had faced an army of invaders, and had realized the hopelessness of his task. He had desperately cried to God, and his petition had been granted. He spoke to the people and said, "Believe in the Lord your God, so shall ye be established; believe his prophets, so shall ye prosper" (2 Chron. 20:20). Then he appointed a choir to lead his troops into battle, "And when they began to sing and to praise, the Lord set ambushments against the children of Ammon, Moab, and Mount Seir . . . and they were smitten" (v. 22). Jehoshaphat went forth to collect the spoils of war, but he was a stupid man! He continued to stare at the treasure, and the gold dust entered his veins.

A Great Fool Slipping

"And after this did Jehoshaphat king of Judah join himself with Ahaziah king of Israel, who did wickedly: and he joined himself with him to make ships to go to Tarshish: and they made the ships in Ezion-gaber" (vv.

35, 36). Unless a man abides in the shadow of the Almighty, the possession of much money can be dangerous. At first the king of Judah refused to enter into a pact with the king of Israel, for the ancient writer has said, "Jehoshaphat made ships of Tarshish to go to Ophir for gold . . . Then said Ahaziah the son of Ahab unto Jehoshaphat, Let my servants go with thy servants in the ships. But Jehoshaphat would not " (1 Kings 22:48, 49). This earlier refusal was, however, followed by an acceptance of the offer of help, and soon the workers were very busy in the shipyards of Ezion-gaber. Slowly a splendid navy began to take shape, and the entire nation spoke of the expedition soon to set sail in search of the gold of Ophir. Poor Jehoshaphat! He had forgotten the advice of the wise man, " My son, if sinners entice thee, consent thou not " (Prov. 1:10).

A Great Fleet Sinking

" Then Eliezer the son of Dodavah of Mareshah prophesied against Jehoshaphat, saying, Because thou hast joined thyself with Ahaziah, the Lord hath broken thy works " (2 Chron. 20:37). Probably Ahaziah smiled at the prediction, for no prophet should interfere with his plans. And if Jehoshaphat felt afraid, he had not the courage to renounce his unholy alliance. Thus the scene was set for the greatest shipping disaster of the ancient world. The gathering crowds had little idea of the impending tragedy as they filled the streets on that colourful day. The men whose skill had created the ships patiently waited to cheer as their vessels sailed toward the horizon. Only the prophet of God remained pensive and sad. The cheering broke out afresh as the royal friends gave their blessing to the expedition; but suddenly, with devastating fury, a tempest came to drive the great vessels to destruction. The plunging ships carried Jehoshaphat's hopes and reputation to the bed of the ocean, and he never recovered from the shock of that awful catastrophe. God removed him from high office, and soon a funeral procession made its way through the streets of his capital city. The expedition had been ruinous. He had forgotten that a poor king can be happier than a wealthy corpse!

EZRA . . . who refused to be swayed by sentiment (Ezra 2:62)

The flags were flying among the Babylonian hovels, for the impossible dream of the captives had come true: their slavery had terminated. Every hour fresh rumours were circulating among the dismal homes, and the young men's enthusiasm seemed boundless. Their revered leader Ezra was actively engaged in high level conferences, and it seemed evident that once the chaotic conditions of the conquered city were under control, emancipation would become a reality. Many of the younger people had been born in captivity, but older folk remembered a little of the bygone days, and sighed at the thought of their homegoing. Then came the news that the final arrangements had been made, and each family was commanded to report at the registration offices.

An Undisturbed Complacency

"And the children of the priests: the children of Habaiah, the children of Koz, the children of Barzillai; which took a wife from the daughters of Barzillai the Gileadite, and were called after their name. These sought their register among those that were reckoned by genealogy, *but they were not found: therefore were they, as polluted, put from the priesthood*" (Ezra 2: 61, 62). And the unexpected disturbance around the registration booth surely caused a great amount of unpleasantness. The great leader refused to be swayed by sentiment, and neither argument nor tears could move him from his determination to reject these applicants. Their claim to belong to the priesthood had been most sincere; but the records of Israel had been faithfully kept, and in these could be found no mention of their names. The leader said that he was very sorry, but the families would have to stand aside until higher authorities could be consulted. What a pity these folk had not ascertained beforehand whether or not their claims could be substantiated. They had lived among the people of God, and had assumed that their names were entered in the records. Now, when it was too late to remedy matters, they had discovered their great mistake. And in like manner, people today assume all will be well in the day of judgment, and yet never attempt to ascertain whether their hopes are based on reliable facts.

An Unsupported Claim

What reply would be made when Ezra enquired, " Why did you not assure yourselves in days gone by that your claims could be substantiated? " Probably they shrugged their shoulders and made excuses. Charles Haddon Spurgeon is credited with the statement, " There will be three outstanding wonders in heaven. (i) People will be present whom I never expected to find. (ii) People will be absent whom I did expect to find. (iii) The greatest wonder will be that I shall be there." Perhaps we could add to the list and say, " There will be many people absent *who expected to be there*." Supposition that all will be well at the termination of life's journey can be totally misleading and disappointing. Concerning the final assize, the Bible declares that all whose names are not found in the Lamb's book of life will be rejected (Rev. 20: 11-15). " The Lord knoweth them that are His," and the names of all His people are recorded in the great book. A man should never rest until he is assured that this important matter has been satisfactorily concluded.

An Unexpected Catastrophe

". . . therefore were they, as polluted, put from the priesthood." The Scriptures are silent concerning any further investigation which may or may not have been made. It is not impossible that further research brought additional evidence to light, and that the tragedy of rejection was ultimately averted. On the other hand, such evidence may not have been forthcoming, and the disappointment of the rejected families would then have been overwhelming. And this is a reminder of the greater issues at stake in the salvation of men and women. There are many people who live and work among Christians, who yet never worry about making their own decision for Christ. They live complacently from day to day, satisfied with the assumption that all must be well. Yet the Scriptures declare that unless their names are recorded in heaven, their most sincere expectation will end in disappointment. The journey into eternity demands preparation, and to neglect this urgent matter is to run the risk of losing everything of value both in this world and in the world to come.

NEHEMIAH . . . who wondered why his choir had disappeared (NEHEMIAH 13:10)

Nehemiah was due for a shock; but in blissful ignorance of what lay ahead, he returned to the land of his fathers. He was pleased, for nearly thirteen years previously the king of Babylon had granted aid whereby Jerusalem had been restored, the wall of the city built again, and the services of the temple recommenced. Nehemiah had been the champion of Israel's cause, and through divine help had been able to overcome the opposition of his enemies. Then duty demanded his return to Babylon, and "in the two and thirtieth year of Artaxerxes king of Babylon came he unto the king, and after certain days obtained leave of the king" (Neh. 13:6). The proud ruler of Babylon was pleased with the gratitude of this trustworthy Israelite, and after hearing news of the prosperity of the project, he gave to Nehemiah further leave of absence.

The House of Surprise

"And I came to Jerusalem, and understood of the evil that Eliashib did for Tobiah, in preparing him a chamber in the courts of the house of the Lord . . . And I perceived that the portion of the Levites had not been given them: for the Levites and the singers, that did the work, were fled every one to his field. Then contended I with the rulers, and said, Why is the house of God forsaken?" (vv. 7-11). Nehemiah had smiled in happy anticipation as he drew near to the house of God, but the continued silence, and the apparent desolation, signified that something had gone wrong with the temple ritual. Something had interfered with the radiant progress of the spiritual life of the city. He entered within the precincts of the sanctuary, and gasped in amazement when he discovered that the place had become a residence for Tobiah the enemy of God and of Israel. Actuated by unknown motives, Eliashib had reached agreement with this enemy, whereby open hostilities ceased as he came to reside in the house of God. This had been a fatal move, for no temple can be filled with the glory of God when the devil lives in its vestry!

The House of Starvation

"And I perceived that the portion of the Levites had not

been given them." When evil had been allowed to lodge in the sacred place, the bringing of tithes to the priests had been neglected. Men lived to please themselves, and even the sanctity of the sabbath had been forgotten. The holy day became a day of trading, and from all parts of the country people brought their produce to turn Jerusalem into a vast market. Even the high priest had condoned sin, for his grandson had married the daughter of Sanballat the Horonite (Neh. 13:28). The poor example given by the rulers led Israel further into sin, for mixed marriages became the popular custom. The Levites were deprived of their food, and had sought a living elsewhere. Thus the bread of life was no longer dispensed in the temple, and soon Tobiah had the place to himself. Surely he laughed at the stupidity of these Israelites. He had failed on the battlefield, but " he who lives and runs away, lives to fight another day." He went away a hated enemy; he returned as an angel of light. He masked his evil heart with a smile, and the priest welcomed him with open arms. Poor Eliashib!

The House of Silence

As the arrogant voice of the invader sounded throughout the sanctuary, discord came to the choir stalls. The songs of God cannot harmonise with the voice of wickedness. Thus the singers took to their heels and fled. The ominous silence which fell upon the house cried aloud for investigation, and as Nehemiah entered the place, his frowns revealed the questionings of his heart. " What had gone wrong? " When he had made preliminary investigations and understood what had taken place, holy fire filled his righteous soul, and he dealt ruthlessly with the hindrances. "And it grieved me sore: therefore I cast forth all the household stuff of Tobiah out of the chamber . . . And one of the sons of Joiada, the son of Eliashib the high priest, was son in law to Sanballat the Horonite: *therefore I chased him from me."* " Faint heart never won fair lady," and neither did compromising heart ever win God's blessing. Indwelling sin is disastrous in the temple of God, and " Know ye not that ye are the temple of God?" (1 Cor. 3:16).

Let us use our temple vestry for prayer meetings, and there will be no room for Tobiah's furniture.

MORDECAI . . . who kept his head by using it

The book of Esther is the one book in the Bible where the name of God is unmentioned, yet nowhere is divine over-ruling so evident as in this ancient story. Constantly we are reminded of the glorious fact that, although God may seem to be absent, He is never far from His people. The chief character in this wonderful account is the heroine queen Esther; but the guiding genius behind every act is Mordecai—the man who kept his head by using it.

God Seeing

" Now in Shushan the palace there was a certain Jew, whose name was Mordecai . . . Who had been carried away from Jerusalem with the captivity . . . And he brought up Hadassah, that is Esther, his uncle's daughter: for she had neither father nor mother, and the maid was fair and beautiful; whom Mordecai, when her father and mother were dead, took for his own daughter " (Esther 2:5-7). Surely, this magnificent act of kindness was well-pleasing to God. He who cares for the fatherless and the widow, probably implanted within the mind of Mordecai the desire to adopt the bereaved orphan. And so God commenced to prepare for the day when Israel would need a saviour. Elsewhere in the Scriptures God has promised, " Before they call, I will answer " (Isa. 65:24), and this is a classic example of that great promise.

God Suggesting

After the dethronement of queen Vashti, the king began to seek for her successor, and the search created excitement throughout the land. The most attractive of Babylon's maidens had to be presented at court, and in order to make this possible, emissaries went in search of candidates. "And Esther was brought also to the king's house, to the custody of Hegai, keeper of the women. And the maiden pleased him, and she obtained kindness of him . . . Esther had not shewed her people nor her kindred: for Mordecai had charged her that she should not shew it " (2:8-10). Mordecai's actions were unpredictable, for not only was this an act of presumption; it was against the entire teachings of Israel that a Jewess should seek marriage with a heathen. Yet the urge to send Esther to the palace deepened to conviction, and for better or for worse he committed himself to the plan. And God watched his every movement.

God Smiling

"In those days, while Mordecai sat in the king's gate, two of the king's chamberlains . . . sought to lay hands on the king . . . And the thing was known to Mordecai, who told it unto Esther the queen; and Esther certified the king thereof in Mordecai's name . . . and it was written in the book of the chronicles before the king" (2:21-23). This act of saving a king's life called for reward, yet in some mysterious way the thought never entered the king's mind; and the waiting Jew only smiled! He was satisfied. Later, when God's people were in danger, the monarch was unable to sleep, "and he commanded to bring the book of the records of the chronicles, and they were read before the king" (6:1). Poor Ahasuerus: how he tossed and turned—and all the time God calmly looked down upon the royal bed and smiled! Perhaps He even whispered, "Sorry—but not tonight." Then the frustrated king developed an interest in the national records, and when the servant commenced to read, it happened that he read at the place which spoke of Mordecai's action in saving the king's life. When the listener's eyes opened in wonderment, God smiled again!

God Saving

In the hour of need, Mordecai had appealed to the queen urging her intervention on Israel's behalf. He had been clothed in sackcloth and had fasted, and since these were religious rites, it is certain that he had prayed to God. The great man prayed and worked, and success attended his efforts. The story reveals that on several occasions Esther risked her life; yet she was never in danger, for she lived in the shadow of the Almighty. And when the drama was played to its climax, "Mordecai the Jew was next unto king Ahasuerus, and great among the Jews, and accepted of the multitude of his brethren, seeking the wealth of his people, and speaking peace to all his seed" (10:3). The historian omitted the name of God probably considering that it was unnecessary. God was everywhere in his story, and that would be sufficient!

DAVID . . . and his apple of gold in a picture of silver

(Psalm 23:4)

King Solomon once said, "A word fitly spoken is like apples of gold in pictures of silver" (Prov. 25:11). Probably he had access to his father's writings, and Psalm 23:4 appeared to him as the greatest of all words fitly spoken. As apples of gold in a silver setting, so seemed this great verse amid the magnificent grandeur of the entire psalm.

How Deliberate His Steps . . . "Yea, though I *walk*"

David realized that the end of his earthly journey was quickly approaching, and that soon he would be required to tread the pilgrim path into a new world. Others in a similar position might have become a prey to panic. Fear would have destroyed their confidence and peace. Yet the man of God looked calmly along the road to see the termination of life's long journey. Unruffled, he proceeded one step at a time. His footsteps did not drag; neither did he hasten with false emotionalism. The man who had walked with God for many years continued to do so until the end.

How Discerning His Sight . . . "*through* the valley of the shadow."

A small window may become a lookout to an entire world. And this proposition is a window through which we are able to see the extent of the psalmist's vision. He did not speak of walking *in* the valley, or even of walking *to* the valley. He said, "Yea, though I walk *through* the valley." His destination lay beyond it, and his was a pilgrim's path. Death was not a termination on life's journey; it was more like a junction where the traveller changed from mortality to immortality in order to continue the journey into higher and grander scenery.

How Decided His Soul . . . "the valley of the *shadow* of death."

Shadows are harmless. They may appear to be very frightening, and many nervous people may shrink in dread before them. Yet the fact remains that a shadow will not hurt anyone. The shadow of a dog will not bite, nor will the shadow of a tree hurt any upon whom it is cast. David realized that he would not be passing through the clutches of the monster called death; his pathway merely ran through its shadow. Shadows are not possible unless a light is shining somewhere, and this shadow was cast across the valley by the Light of the World, who was waiting to welcome the homecoming pilgrim.

How Delivered His Spirit . . . " I will fear no evil "

" Perfect love casteth out fear," and David loved the Lord with all his heart. Oppression was unknown in his spirit, for communion had transformed his outlook. There had been days when he had been forced to cry, " Why art thou cast down, O my soul? Hope thou in God: for I shall yet praise him " (Psa. 42:5). But now, all such experiences belonged to the past. A perfect peace had settled upon his soul; a calm had banished unrest from his mind: all was well.

How Dependable His Saviour . . . " for thou art with me."

David's history had been rather chequered. His best friends had failed him, and on two occasions members of his own family had threatened his life. Yet in spite of these distressing events, he had continually known the companionship of his God. In all the changing scenes of life, the Lord had been true to His covenant promises; and now that death was near, the psalmist had no doubt that God would be with him in the valley.

How Delightful His Song . . . " thy rod and thy staff they comfort me."

And so, once again, David remembered the days of his childhood, when as a shepherd boy he had owned both rod and staff. Resolutely he had protected his flock; gently he had reproved the obstinate of his sheep; and every day he had led them to new pastures and sparkling waters. He smiled as he wrote, " The Lord is my shepherd; I shall not want." Eternal love had been manifested in all God's dealings. As David had cared for his flock, so the great Shepherd loved every human sheep. The psalmist meditated upon these sublime facts, and as comfort flooded his soul he exclaimed, " Surely goodness and mercy shall follow me all the days of my life: and I will dwell in the house of the Lord for ever."

DAVID . . . and the madness which suggested a psalm
(PSALM 34: 6-8; 1 SAMUEL 21:13)

David sat in the cave of Adullum and quietly watched the surrounding countryside. The days were perilous, and a price had been placed on his head. Away through the trees, rugged men guarded the trails; in the secrecy of their stronghold, other men prepared a meal; but all the while their brave young leader dreamed and watched. In thought he still saw the hazardous flight into the country of Gath, and he involuntarily shuddered as he recalled the narrowness of his escape in that foreign land. David smiled when he remembered his desperate acting. In retrospect it appeared strangely comical; but then, grim tragedy had stalked his every movement. The enemies had watched as he clawed at the walls; they had frowned with disgust as his spittle ran down his beard; and the immature actor had been forced to better displays of theatricals. He had traced fantastic patterns on the walls, and his laughs had been those of an idiot. His actions had been grotesque and revolting, and finally his enemies had pronounced him insane. They had driven the lunatic away, but had failed to see the relief which suddenly appeared in his eyes. David took his writing material, lifted his face to the sky, and as gratitude filled his soul he wrote Psalm 34.

David's Great Salvation

Slowly he wrote his testimony—"This poor man cried, and the Lord heard him, and saved him out of all his troubles." Maybe he paused awhile and put down his pen, for he realized that statement fitted many episodes in his eventful career. The words "This poor man" seem to indicate that every vestige of David's self-confidence had disappeared before an overwhelming sense of personal need. Desperately he had cried to God for help, and his petition had been heard.

Verse 6 suggests a proposition. *A man must recognize his need before God can save him.* This is one of the basic laws of Holy Scripture and human experience. When a man has unlimited confidence in his own ability, he feels no need for God. A sense of insufficiency begets a desire to pray, and prayer is the key which unlocks heaven's resources.

David's Great Security

David's pen is moving again. " The angel of the Lord encampeth round about them that fear him, and delivereth them." Once again the scenes of recent days appeared before David's eyes. But for the explanation provided by his own words, how else could he have escaped from his enemies? King Saul was probably an expert javelin thrower; but in any case, a child could not have missed a sitting target at that distance. David had been playing at Saul's feet. Then the escape from Gath had been most providential. That a one-time shepherd boy should without rehearsal develop into a first-rate actor seemed impossible. Even David could scarcely believe his own memories. Surely in his successive hours of need, the angel of the Lord had encamped round him. God had been his refuge and strength, a very present help in trouble. Verse 7 suggests another proposition. *God is never far from a man who is needing help.* And that is as true today as it was in David's day.

David's Great Satisfaction

" O taste and see that the Lord is good: blessed is the man that trusteth in him." The story of testimony halts as this spontaneous expression of praise rises unchecked from a thankful heart. God had been exceedingly kind and gracious, and David knew the blessedness of the man whose trust is in the Lord. Eventually, before he laid aside his pen, he wrote, ". . . none of them that trust in Him shall be desolate."

The birds were singing in the trees, and the sun, a ball of flaming glory, had filled the sky with crimson. The evening meal was ready, and the men were waiting. David stood up. He was a prince indeed, for his meditation had taken him into the presence of the eternal King. Yes, all was well . . . and he went to join his followers. In thought we watch him; and then, recalling his third great statement, we recognize our final proposition. *Concerning the things of God, to taste for a moment means to trust for ever.*

THE WISE MAN . . . and his baffling problems

Paul declared, " But the natural man receiveth not the things of the Spirit of God: for they are foolishness unto him: neither can he know them, because they are spiritually discerned " (1 Cor. 2:14). The experiences of the Christian are essentially spiritual, and as such they are beyond the comprehension of the unregenerate man. This fact is illustrated in the testimony of the ancient philosopher who confessed his inability to understand the ways of creation. He said, " There be three things which are too wonderful for me, yea, four which I know not; the way of an eagle in the air; the way of a serpent upon a rock; the way of a ship in the midst of the sea; and the way of a man with a maid." A fundamental principle of the Christian faith is expressed in each of these word-pictures.

The Problem of a Man Trusting

There are many interesting details about the habits of the eagle, but the greatest of all is the method by which the young are taught to fly. The nest is usually built at the top of an inaccessible mountain, where there is little danger of interference. When the young birds are old enough to fly, the parent bird ruthlessly destroys the nest and pushes her offspring over the side of the precipice. Then, as the young eaglets are fluttering helplessly downwards, the mother bird swoops to catch the chicks on her wings. And in the repetition of this process, the frightened birds desperately spread and flap their wings, and ultimately make the astonishing discovery that by so doing they are able to arrest the downward urge and to follow their mother toward the blue sky. That scene illustrates the problem of the young man learning to trust God. He may hear the Gospel and feel inclined to believe its promises, but it is only when he launches out in faith, trusting that God will care for him, that he discovers " underneath are the everlasting arms."

The Problem of a Man Holding

The serpent has neither hands nor feet with which to climb, yet in some uncanny fashion it reaches precipitous places where man is unable to go. The ancient thinker had obviously marvelled at the way the serpent could take hold of the rock. All creation abounds with similar characteristics. The fly can walk on the ceiling, and for no apparent reason, stay there when all else would fall. The limpet clings to the rocks at the sea shore, and even the greatest waves are unable to dislodge it. And the secret of all these miracles is suction. The serpent takes hold of the rock, and the rock takes hold of the serpent, and with no foreign elements coming between, either one holds the other. So it is with the young Christian. Great cliffs of difficulty may block his path, and conscious of his own inherent weakness he may feel inclined to despair. Yet God's strength will be made perfect in his weakness when he learns to cling to the Rock of Ages.

The Problem of a Man Advancing

Huge ocean-going liners were unknown in Old Testament days, and sea-faring men had to depend upon sailing ships. They quickly learned that the set of the sails and not the force of the wind governed their direction. Even though the winds seemed adverse, they could be used to good account by the skilful manipulation of the picturesque sheets of canvas high above their heads. And this is also true of the greater experiences of life. There are times when circumstances would drive our souls to the rocks of destruction; but the man whose heart is inclined toward the Lord will have his sails set in such a fashion that even the ill winds will be made to work together for his good.

The Problem of a Man Loving

"The way of a man with a maid." Love can make a selfish man considerate of others. Love can make a strong man weak. Love—real love for a sweetheart—will lead a man to sacrifice in a way hitherto unknown in his experience. Love can do almost anything. This is the great secret behind every experience of the Christian. It enables us to trust Christ; to cling to Christ; and to allow His hand to control us even amid the wildest storms of life. Perfect love casteth out fear. The heart can solve problems which baffle the intellect, for "love never faileth."

THE WALL BREAKERS . . . who were bitten by serpents

". . . whoso breaketh an hedge (a wall), a serpent shall bite him." This is one of the wisest of all the proverbs of Solomon. Let us first notice that there are three living agencies in the verse. (i) *Someone willing to build.* Neither wall nor hedge comes into being by accident. (ii) *Someone wanting to break.* (iii) *Something waiting to bite.* Job 1:9, 10 is a most illuminating commentary on this text. "Then Satan answered the Lord, and said, Doth Job fear God for nought? Hast thou not built an hedge (wall) about him? . . ." Thus the builder of the wall is God; the unwise wrecker of the wall is man; and the enemy waiting to bite is Satan. ". . . whoso breaketh God's wall, Satan shall bite him." In all kinds of ways the Lord has placed a wall around His people.

The Wall of God's Great Law

"And it shall come to pass, if thou shalt hearken diligently unto the voice of the Lord thy God, to observe and to do all his commandments which I command thee this day, that the Lord thy God will set thee on high above all nations of the earth . . . But it shall come to pass, if thou wilt not hearken unto the voice of the Lord thy God . . . that all these curses shall come upon thee" (Deut. 28:1, 15). The ten commandments were a wall of protection to Israel. They were warned that if they foolishly broke the wall, disaster would inevitably follow. When the prophet Jeremiah ministered to the nation, he reminded them of all these things, but his words were rejected (Jer. 17:21-23). Israel decided to break the wall of God, and as they did so they discovered a Babylonian serpent was waiting to bite them (Psa. 137:1).

The Walls of a Godly Home

"And Jesus said, A certain man had two sons: and the younger of them said to his father, Father, give me the portion of goods that falleth to me. And he divided unto them his living. And not many days after the younger son gathered all together, and took his journey into a far country . . ." (Luke 15:12, 13). The Prodigal broke through the protection thrown around him by the kindly restrictions of his home, and in less time than it takes to tell, a serpent had bitten him. Destitute and despairing, he was forced to seek food among the swine, and no man had pity on him. Perhaps it could be said of him, " By the swine troughs of a far country, he sat down and wept when he remembered Zion." We sometimes quote the proverb " A stitch in time, saves nine." It would be equally true to say that a tear in time saves untold heartaches. And if the ordinary home be a protection to a child, how much more is this the case when we think of the Church. It is there that the family of God meets together; it is there that His sons and daughters listen to the Father's voice. If any backsliding Christian should break through that wall to search for illegitimate pleasures, the serpents of the far country will bite him.

The Wall of Conscience

The greatest wall ever to be erected by God was the wall of conscience. Within every human being is a watchful monitor whose attentions can become most troublesome. A man may know little of the laws of God, and may never have experienced the privilege of living within a godly home, yet, whosoever he might be, the third wall is something intimately connected with his life. The Creator has given to him a conscience, that he might be kept in a place of safety. Let a man break this wall, and a serpent will soon bite him. Mark, the amanuensis of Simon Peter, provides a striking example of this fact. In describing the denial by Peter, he goes on to explain that after the first failure, *" Peter went out into the porch;* and the cock crew "* (Mark 14 : 68). Had the disciple walked out into the night, the greater part of his tragedy would have been averted. Conscience took him to the door, compromise stopped him there. Slowly he went back to the warmth of the fireside, and in so doing he broke through God's wall and was bitten twice in quick succession. " And Peter went out, and wept bitterly " (Luke 22 : 62). The man who meddles and unnecessarily destroys a wall, asks for trouble. He will need much more than his tears to destroy the venom of a serpent bite. To be forewarned is to be forearmed.

ISAIAH . . . the prophet who wrote a Bible

The authorship of the book of Isaiah has caused a great amount of animated discussion in every section of the Church. It is common knowledge that the tone of the first thirty-nine chapters is entirely different from that of the concluding twenty-seven chapters, and this fact has supported many scholars in their affirmation that at least two men were responsible for this remarkable book. It is not our purpose now to discuss the relative merits of any such theory, for greater issues are waiting to be examined. The book itself is far more important than any question of authorship, and this fact becomes increasingly evident when we discover it to be a miniature Bible.

Isaiah's Old and New Testaments

The difference in tone and theme occurs after the thirty-ninth chapter. Prior to that point, God's great judgments provide the theme of the author. Sin is seen to be the great enemy of the nation, and upon it God pours His wrath. Without warning the next chapter begins with a new message. "Comfort ye, comfort ye my people, saith your God." Then for twenty-seven chapters, the prophecy speaks of the grace of God. Scholars have found these sections incompatible with the idea that one man's pen was responsible for the entire book. Yet the greatest fact of all is that here so clearly we are able to see the two sections of the Scriptures. Isaiah's thirty-nine chapters of law represent the Old Testament. His closing twenty-seven chapters represent the equivalent number of books in the New Testament. The comparison is too noticeable to be a coincidence.

Isaiah's " Gospels " and " Acts of the Apostles "

In this matter the details are really astounding. According to the division suggested, Matthew to Acts would be represented by Isaiah's chapters 40-44. Chapter 40 would represent Matthew's Gospel; 41 would be Mark's Gospel; 42 would be Luke's Gospel; 43 would be equivalent to John's Gospel, and finally, chapter 44 would indicate the Acts of the Apostles. In this connection we can only repeat a statement. The study of these Scriptures will produce facts truly amazing. Matthew's Gospel is the message concerning the Kingship of Jesus. In like manner Isaiah's " New Testament " opens with the ministry of John Baptist, and goes on to say, " Behold, the Lord God will come with strong hand, and his arm shall *rule* for him" (40:10). The following chapter, which would represent Mark's Gospel, emphasizes the fact that the Lord will serve His people and minister to their every need. This, of course, is also true of the second Gospel, where Christ is portrayed as the Servant. Luke revealed the Saviour as " the perfect Man." It is most remarkable that in the corresponding Gospel as written by Isaiah, we are able to read, " The Lord shall go forth as *a mighty man . . .*" (42:13). Chapter 43 stresses the deity of the Saviour, and thus perfectly expresses the message of the fourth Gospel. Over and over again the prophet proclaimed," I am the Lord thy God, the Holy One of Israel, thy Saviour . . ." (v. 3). " I, even I am the Lord; and beside me there is no Saviour " (v. 11). " I am the Lord, your Holy One, the creator of Israel, your King " (v. 15). As a tremendous climax to this strange study, we must note that in chapter 44, Isaiah's Acts of the Apostles, v. 3 says, " For I will pour water upon him that is thirsty, and floods upon the dry ground: I *will pour my Spirit upon thy seed,* and my blessing upon thine offspring." Thus we arrive at Pentecost, where God fulfilled the ancient promise.

Isaiah's Cross of Calvary

The *central* chapter of Isaiah's New Testament would naturally be the fourteenth of the twenty-seven chapters; and to find the exact position of this chapter in the entire book, it is necessary to add the number to the preceding thirty-nine chapters. It follows that the *heart* of Isaiah's New Testament is the fifty-third chapter of the book, where we read: " But he was wounded for our transgressions, he was bruised for our iniquities: the chastisement of our peace was upon him; and with his stripes we are healed " (v. 5).

It seems the height of folly to argue about the identity of an author when the writings offer so much food for thought. Surely the Lord over-ruled in all things, in order to demonstrate that His word is *one* word—eternally settled in the heavens.

HEZEKIAH . . . who asked God to read a letter

(Isaiah 37:14) 3/7/87

The position was desperate, and the defenders of the city trembled with fear. They were brave men, but it had become obvious that the enemy was too strong for them to resist. City after city had fallen before his ceaseless onslaughts, and the legend of his invincibility had spread through the land. Every movement of the heathen horde had been reported to Hezekiah, but vain had been the hope that the tide of evil would recede. Sennacherib, the king of Assyria, had planned the assault on Jerusalem, and when his armies marched toward the city, the worst fears of king Hezekiah were realized.

Hezekiah's Great Distress. . . . A letter sent out

An arrogant heathen captain stood outside Jerusalem's wall, his armour gleaming in the sunlight. His fierce countenance seemed alight with grim purposeful determination as he shouted, " What confidence is this wherein thou trusteth . . . I will give thee two thousand horses, if thou be able on thy part to set riders upon them " (Isa. 36:4, 8). His rumbling laughter echoed around the wall. The mockery and banter of the Assyrian were revealed again when, with chin fiercely jutting forward, he asked, " How then wilt thou turn away the face of one captain of the least of my master's servants? " (v. 9). Silence reigned among the listeners. It was true that many other cities had fallen, and nothing short of a miracle could save Jerusalem. A little while later a letter was delivered to the king of Israel, and as he read its message, fear increased in his soul. " Let not thy God, in whom thou trustest, deceive thee, saying, Jerusalem shall not be given into the hand of the king of Assyria. Behold thou hast heard what the kings of Assyria have done to all lands by destroying them utterly; and shalt thou be delivered?" (37:10, 11). What could he do? And if other people of today seem to be in a similar predicament, the ancient story might offer advice and comfort.

Hezekiah's Great Desires. . . . A letter spread out

" And Hezekiah received the letter from the hand of the messengers, and read it: and Hezekiah went up unto the house of the Lord, and spread it before the Lord. And Hezekiah prayed unto the Lord, saying . . . Incline thine ear, O Lord, and hear; open thine eyes, O Lord, and see: and hear all the words of Sennacherib, which hath sent to reproach the living God " (vv. 15-17). And surely the God who lived above the mercy seat looked down upon the up-turned face of His troubled servant, and at the same time invisible eyes read the words of challenge so clearly set forth upon the parchment. It is a wise thing to share our problems with God. Earlier, the king had sought the help of Isaiah the prophet, and the warmth of brotherly fellow-ship had cheered his soul. However, in the greater issues of life it is far better to seek direct audience with the Almighty, and not to trust in the solicitations of any human counsellor. The ancient king was a privileged man in being able to approach that altar; yet, all people of this age may know a far greater privilege.

Hezekiah's Great Deliverance . . . A letter blotted out

" Then Isaiah the son of Amoz sent unto Hezekiah, saying, Thus saith the Lord the God of Israel, Whereas thou hast prayed to me against Sennacherib king of Assyria: This is the word which the Lord hath spoken concerning him; The virgin, the daughter of Zion, hath despised thee, and laughed thee to scorn; the daughter of Jerusalem hath shaken her head at thee. . . . I will turn thee back by the way which thou camest. . . . Thou shalt not come into this city, saith the Lord. For I will defend this city to save it for mine own sake, and for my servant David's sake. Then the angel of the Lord went forth, and smote in the camp of the Assyrians a hundred and four-score and five thousand: and when they arose in the morning, behold, they were all dead corpses " (37:21-36). Then the songs of praise were heard again in the city, and the letter of an arrogant king was practically blotted out from the memory of the people. Let us never forget that God is the same " from everlasting to everlasting " (Psa. 90:2). We can draw near to share our problems with a heavenly Father. The path of prayer leads to the secret place, and, " He that dwelleth in the secret place of the most High shall abide under the shadow of the Almighty " (Psa. 91:1).

THE POTTER . . . who supplied God with an object lesson
(JEREMIAH 18:1-6)

Jeremiah stood in the doorway of the potter's house, and quietly watched the scene within. With a smile and a word of greeting, the craftsman had turned from the visitor to the wheel upon which his lump of clay was spinning. Placing two thumbs into the centre of the dirty ball, the potter gently pressed the spinning mass, and immediately as though by a miracle, a vessel began to take shape.

A Marred Vessel Can Never Satisfy the Potter *1/30/87*

His reputation would be at stake if he sent imperfect vessels to be sold in the market. Suddenly the wheel ceased to spin; the vessel came to a standstill, and the frown upon the potter's face told of his keen displeasure. Unyielding substances were spoiling his designs, and it was impossible to extract these hindrances without ruining the entire work. Thereupon the potter crushed his vessel, and immediately set about the task of removing the foreign bodies from the clay. Then once again the wheel was set spinning, and the vessel was remade. Long afterward the prophet remembered those moments and wrote, " Then the word of the Lord came to me, saying, O house of Israel, cannot I do with you as this potter? saith the Lord. Behold, as the clay is in the potter's hand, so are ye in mine hand, O house of Israel." God had certainly created His people Israel, but His skill had been hindered by flaws of sin. Unless the people would bend to His will, He would need to crush them and begin again. The ancient message has lessons for today. The Lord has brought His Church into being, and it is His purpose to make it conformable unto His will. Alas, so often sin interferes with the fulfilment of His great plans.

An Unfinished Vessel Can Never Satisfy the Potter

Unless he could complete his task, his past labours would have been in vain. The marred vessel constituted a challenge to the greatness of his skill, and thus he patiently restored it to his wheel and persevered until his labours were brought to a satisfactory conclusion. This prophetic object-lesson is seen in all the writings concerning Israel.

God found it necessary to crush His people, yet, as the divine Potter, He must complete His work on behalf of the nation, or every past effort was a waste of time. And if this be true concerning Israel, it is more so concerning the Church. John declares that when Christ shall appear, we shall be like Him (1 John 3:2). It follows that since heaven demands such a high standard of personal perfection, the Lord must complete the work already commenced in our souls, or His past efforts on our behalf—even the death of the cross—will have been disappointing and in vain.

A Completed Vessel Can Never Satisfy the Potter Unless it is Clean and Ready for Use

Jeremiah watched as the potter proudly slid the vessel from the wheel. The workman was very satisfied, for every blemish had been removed. When the prophet slowly walked away over the fields, he knew he had witnessed the unfolding of one of God's great sermons. " Behold, as the clay is in the potter's hand, so are ye in mine hand, O house of Israel." God desired a clean and useful people. It was His eternal purpose to make Israel the instrument of blessing to a world. Alas, the nation was sinful and unreliable. And so the prophet cried, " O Israel, hear the voice of the Lord your God." The identical message comes to the Church, for unless our blemishes be removed, unless human vessels be moulded according to the will of God, divine graciousness will be frustrated. God can never entrust the sweetness of His Spirit to a vessel filled with flaws; nor can He use unclean instruments. If the saint desires to render fruitful service, he must be conformed to the image of God's Son. Body, mind, and spirit must yield to the pressure of the divine hand, so that God's perfect will might be operative in daily life. Such men have been used of God to save nations; and there is reason to believe that similar miracles could be performed today if Christians were fully yielded to their Master's will.

Have Thine own way, Lord,
  Have Thine own way;
Thou art the Potter
  I am the clay.
Mould me and make me
  After Thy will,
While I am waiting
  Yielded and still.

EBED-MELECH . . . the black man who rescued a prophet

• (JEREMIAH 38:7-13)

They were terrible days in Israel when one lone man fought the battles of the Lord. Unrest and fear had placed a terrifying hand upon the people; and to make matters worse, a Babylonian invasion seemed imminent. Yet the sinful leaders of the nation persisted in their contempt of God's law, and deliberately sought the help of idols. Against this tide of evil the prophet Jeremiah had vainly struggled; and his prediction of impending doom won for him the scorn of his fellow men. They declared that his untimely prophecies were undermining the morale of the defenders, and in order to silence him for ever, they cast him into an old muddy pit which had formerly been used as a dungeon. As he sank into the obnoxious filth, Jeremiah's position became extremely precarious; and then a man of Africa came to the rescue.

A Story of God's Watchfulness

" Now when Ebed-melech the Ethiopian . . . heard that they had put Jeremiah in the dungeon, he went forth out of the king's house, and spake to the king, saying, My lord the king, these men have done evil in all that they have done to Jeremiah the prophet, whom they have cast into the dungeon; and he is likely to die for hunger in the place where he is: for there is no more bread in the city." The intervention of this gallant Ethiopian undoubtedly saved the life of God's servant, and at the same time it endangered his own, for had the noblemen heard of Ebed-melech's interference, their reactions would have been most violent. " Then the king commanded Ebed-melech the Ethiopian, saying, Take from hence thirty men with thee, and take up Jeremiah the prophet out of the dungeon, before he die. So Ebed-melech took the men . . . and old cast clouts and old rotten rags, and let them down by cords into the dungeon to Jeremiah. And he said, Put these . . . under thine armholes under the cords. So they drew up Jeremiah . . . and took him up out of the dungeon." The Almighty watched every movement of the rescue operation, and the account of His rewarding the brave Ethiopian makes good reading.

A Story of God's Thoughtfulness

As the threats of invasion increased, fear spread through the land, and even Ebed-melech was not immune from terror. Rumours of Babylonian savagery played havoc with his peace of mind, and he feared the worst. Then came the word of the Lord to Jeremiah saying, " Go and speak to Ebed-melech the Ethiopian, saying, Thus saith the Lord of hosts, the God of Israel: Behold, I will bring my words upon this city for evil, and not for good; and they shall be accomplished in that day before thee. But I will deliver thee in that day, saith the Lord, and thou shalt not be given into the hand of the men of whom thou art afraid. For I will surely deliver thee . . . because thou hast put thy trust in me, saith the Lord " (Jer. 39:16-18). When the anxious man received this message, his confidence was restored. He realized that God's word was true; and although a thousand might fall at his side, and ten thousand at his right hand, the destruction would not harm him. God knew the state of His servant's mind, and with thoughtfulness characteristic of His unfailing care, took steps to restore the peace of His subject.

A Story of God's Faithfulness

When Jerusalem was overrun, the helpless people surely thought their world had come to an end. Arrogant Gentiles stalked through the holy places; blasphemy raised its ugly head to mock the cause of Israel, and everywhere defenders lay dead or dying. The eerie silence of the stricken city was broken only by the coarse jests of the conquerors, as captives assembled to march toward the slavery of a foreign land. Truly the prophet's word had been fulfilled. Yet in some mysterious fashion the Babylonian king recognized and respected the greatness of the prophet Jeremiah, and made provision for his safety. *The historian Josephus records how the prophet's request brought liberty once again to his own servant Baruch, and probably in the same manner, freedom was obtained for the brave African who had earlier risked his life to rescue God's minister. The Lord is no man's debtor, and happy indeed is that soul who receives his rewards from God's hand. Even a poor man may be confident if he be a friend of the divine Banker.

---

* Antiquities of the Jews, by Flavius Josephus: Book 10, Chapter 9, Para 1.

THE VOICE . . . which interrupted three great meetings

(MATTHEW 3:17)

All true preaching begins in heaven. From thence come the living word, the power of the Holy Spirit, and the blessing of the Almighty; and without these the most eloquent of men are but tinkling cymbals. All who would testify of the Saviour should take as their example the three occasions when God preached from His cloudy pulpit. At the beginning, in the middle, and again at the conclusion of His earthly ministry, God bore witness concerning His Son; and these Scriptures form a comprehensive commentary on the Person of Christ.

God Witnessed concerning the Purity of His Son
    (Matt. 3:16-17)

When John Baptist first appeared in the Jordan valley, few people could have visualized the scenes soon to take place. The peaceful countryside soon became filled with eager listeners, and the baptismal services eloquently told of the power of John's ministry. One day Jesus of Nazareth came to be baptized, and as the crowd watched, " The Spirit of God descended like a dove . . . upon him: And lo a voice from heaven, saying, This is my beloved Son, in whom I am well pleased." In order to appreciate the magnitude of this statement, we must remember that sin is a nature. Before Adam could sin, it was necessary for Satan to tempt him. Yet later, when Cain murdered his brother, the wicked thought originated in his own being. The entrance of sin into Adam's life had made him a sinner; and that life was transmitted to his child. Thus did David say, " Behold, I was shapen in iniquity; and in sin did my mother conceive me " (Psa. 51:5). Without the miraculous conception, Jesus of Nazareth would have been born a sinner. Christ resisted every temptation, and at the beginning of His public ministry God was able to say, " This is my beloved Son, in whom I am well pleased."

God Witnessed concerning the Preaching of His Son
    (Matt. 17:5)

"And behold a voice out of the cloud, which said, This is my beloved Son, in whom I am well pleased; *hear ye him."* By the addition of a single sentence, God increased the scope of His testimony concerning the Lord Jesus. Amid all the contradictory statements and confusion in Israel, God instructed the leaders of the Church to heed the words of the Saviour. As the living Word, He was the expression of the highest authority; no earthly wisdom could supersede His knowledge of the counsels and purposes of God. His teaching concerning the fundamental things of time and eternity was fully endorsed by God, and the greatest advice ever given to preachers was enshrined in "hear ye him." That Christ was termed the Son of God did not signify that He was less than the Father. Christ is called the Son to reveal that He is of the same essence: not to signify His inferiority, but as an indication of oneness in the divine Family.

God Witnessed concerning the Passion of His Son
(John 12:28)

As the shadow of the cross began to darken the horizon of Jesus, His soul became troubled and He said, "What shall I say? Father, save me from this hour: but for this cause came I unto this hour. Father, glorify thy name. Then came there a voice from heaven, saying, I have both glorified it, and will glorify it again . . . Jesus answered (the people) and said, This voice came not because of me, but for your sakes . . . I, if I be lifted up from the earth, will draw all men unto me" (vv. 27-32). Thus did God speak beforehand concerning the death of His Son. The tragedy of the cross was to become the greatest triumph of all time, the medium whereby the Father would be glorified, and the Son eternally exalted as the supreme head of His redeemed people. Calvary was destined to become a lighthouse to guide life's travellers to an everlasting harbour of refuge. No one can dispute the fulfilment of the Saviour's word, for the power of redeeming love represents the greatest force in our world. The Lord Jesus Christ occupied the supreme place in the affections of God; and if He be relegated to any other position in my heart, then my folly will rival the love of God in dimensions.

THE SAVIOUR . . . and His strangest utterance

(MATTHEW 10:34-36)

The coming of Christ stirred the hearts of Israel as they had never previously been stirred, and from all parts of the country crowds rushed to hear the new Teacher. Every miracle gave promise of greater things to come, and the fact that He gave peace to innumerable sufferers seemed to guarantee that soon He would be able to bring peace to the troubled nation. Then to the consternation of His followers, He said, "Think not that I am come to send peace on earth: I came not to send peace but a sword. For I am come to set a man at variance against his father, and the daughter against her mother . . . And a man's foes shall be they of his own household."

The Sword that Wounds

The Bible has three things to say of the usefulness of a sword. In the first place, it is able to wound. The Saviour came to act as a great surgeon, and knowing the need of His patients, He liberated a Gospel destined to be a two-edged sword. Recognizing the deep-seated need of sinners, the Lord Jesus did not hesitate to hurt them, for only by so doing could He hope to bring healing to their sick hearts. He also warned His disciples that the forceful presentation of the Gospel message would arouse resentment, for the sword of truth would penetrate into the secret places of the conscience to reveal those things that most people would prefer to remain hidden. He said, "Woe unto you, when all men shall speak well of you!" (Luke 6:26). Holy warfare must always precede the healing of souls, for until sin is ruthlessly exposed and overcome, spiritual healing will be an impossibility.

The Sword that Separates

"For I am come to set a man at variance against his father, and the daughter against her mother," and we might add "a friend against his friend." The incoming of the Gospel message leads to a complete transformation in the outlook of men. The convert's former associates will probably misunderstand his motives, and might even persecute him in the new faith. In order to follow the

Lord Jesus, the Christian may have to renounce his old delights and forsake many of his former friends. The business man may find it necessary to revise all his ideas of trading, and if this should lead to serious financial loss his partners will probably have a great deal to say in the matter. A wife who has accepted Christ as her Saviour may find it impossible to accompany her husband in the ways of sin, and her refusal to co-operate may lead to domestic unpleasantness. The sword of the Gospel will sever ties that might have been in existence for years, and instead of creating peace, will prove to be the harbinger of discord. The early history of the Church provided ample evidence of the truth of Christ's prediction.

The Sword that Ministers

The inspired Old Testament prophet recognized another use for the sword, and embodied his vision in his thrilling utterance concerning the coming of the King. "And he shall judge among the nations, and shall rebuke many people: and they shall beat their swords into ploughshares, and their spears into pruning hooks: nation shall not lift up sword against nation, neither shall they learn war any more" (Isa. 2:4). The prophet saw that the coronation of the Messiah would transform the steel weapons of war and make them to serve a new purpose in the production of food. People who had been hurt by the sword would suddenly be fed by the new instrument. And in like manner, this is true concerning the Gospel of Christ. The message of redemption will hurt, and then separate the sinner from the ways of sin. Yet when this operation has been completed, and Christ occupies the throne of a man's affection, the Bible suddenly becomes the greatest book in the world, for within its pages the Christian discovers the true source of the bread of life. It will minister to his deepest needs, and satisfy his hungry soul. The universal coronation of the Lord Jesus will lead to a new world, and the greatest proof of this sublime fact is found when a similar transformation takes place within the kingdom of a man's heart.

PETER . . . whose ardour was somewhat damped (Matthew 14:25-33)

Simon Peter did many praiseworthy things during the course of his lifetime, but this episode of walking upon the water must rank as one of the greatest. When fear had frayed his nervous energies, and when a seeming apparition had startled the entire crew, the realisation that the Saviour had drawn near was a little too much for Peter's self-control. In the excitement and relief of the moment he cried, " Lord, if it be thou, bid me come unto thee on the water. And Jesus said, Come. And when Peter was come down out of the ship, he walked on the water, to go to Jesus."

A Triumphant Response

We must never under-estimate the greatness of Peter's achievement. Surrounded by obvious dangers, and faced with utter impossibilities, Peter found strength in his Lord's command; and forgetting all else, he stepped into the midst of a noisy tempest. *And he did not sink.* It seems fitting that this should have happened to Peter, for in later days he was destined to be the evangelist of the Church. Few pictures could so aptly reveal the beginning of a Christian journey. When Christ draws near to the tempest-tossed souls of men and women, the sound of His voice brings life's greatest challenge. Eventually the soul is confronted by the call to leave a comparatively safe boat in order to step into the unknown. Reason and doubt would shrink from this; but a burning heart, an eager soul, and a waiting Christ are very hard to deny.

A Terrible Reality

The story presents no difficulties to the man who has responded to a similar invitation. The facts of Christian experience prove that no man was ever engulfed by temptation while he steadfastly looked at his Saviour. Through His enabling grace, it is possible to trample under foot the very waves that would bury us. Yet even the greatest saint is endangered when he loses sight of his Lord. " But when Peter saw the wind boisterous, he was afraid; and beginning to sink . . . " Frantic despair gripped the sinking man as he cried, " Lord, save me." Possibly he thought he had been unwise to leave the boat; but in later years, saner judgment admitted that the mistake lay in losing sight of his Lord. When he ceased listening to and looking at his Master, dangers overcame him.

A Trembling Request

Peter's prayer is one of the best on record. There are no superfluous words, and no unnecessary finesse of phraseology. It is the quickest, easiest, and most desperate way of reaching the heart of God. " Lord, save me." His sudden cry reveals three vital things. (i) *His predicament.* He was sinking, and every moment counted if he were to be saved from drowning. (ii) *His perception.* Christ was near, and was able to save. The ability of the Master more than equalled the demands of the moment. If only He *would,* He *could* meet Peter's need. (iii) *His Prayer.* There was no time to elaborate any details, and no time to observe any ceremonial law. One thing mattered, and that was to be saved. It banished all else from Peter's mind, and he cried, " Lord, save me." This modern world would be well advised to emulate Peter's example.

A Timely Reply

" And immediately Jesus stretched forth his hand, and caught him, and said unto him, O thou of little faith, wherefore didst thou doubt? " The surging waves gave up their victim, and as Peter instinctively wiped the water from his eyes, he realized that once again he was standing on the sea. The boat was some distance away, but fear had now disappeared. A new calm had settled upon his mind, for he was conscious that Christ still held his hand. His clothing was saturated with water, but every moment, increasing elation drove the chill from his spirits. Yes, he could walk on the water that would have drowned him. Maybe in after years Paul gave to Peter a text to fit the occasion. " I can do all things through Christ which strengtheneth me " (Phil. 4:13). The secret of every Christian triumph seems to be expressed in the two words: "*through Christ.*"

> Hold thou my hand: so weak I am and helpless;
> I dare not go one step without Thy aid.
> Hold Thou my hand: for then, O loving Saviour,
> No dread of ill shall make my soul afraid.

PETER . . . and his greatest fishing story

Simon Peter was worried. He had a cloud on his mind, and a shadow had fallen across his soul. The Master had discovered his problem, and had sent him on a fishing expedition. Peter was glad to get away from the searching eyes of the Lord; but his problem remained. Slowly he went down to the edge of the waves; he baited his hook, and with a dexterous twist of his wrist, sent his sinker skimming over the water. Thoughtfully he watched the splash, and allowing the line to slip through his fingers, waited until its slackness told that the sinker was at the bottom. Slowly he wound in the line until it was moderately taut, and then he waited. Eventually the telltale wriggle of the handline informed him that the bait had been attractive, and with long steady pulls he hauled in his fish. Peter gripped it with his free hand, and then prizing the hook from its mouth, he nonchalantly looked at the coin between the jaws of his captive. As he placed it safely in his pocket, he turned and walked up the beach.

The Man with a Cloud on his Mind

His troubles had begun when the income tax officials had asked him, " Doth not your Master pay tribute? " (Matt. 17:24). Spontaneously, Simon answered, " Yes," but afterward he wondered if he had told the truth; if he were guilty of defrauding the authorities; if they would investigate the matter, and bring punishment upon the disciple band. Finally his countenance shewed evidence of his great concern. When he did not bring his troubles to the Lord, his worry increased. The Lord Jesus recognized the symptoms of anxiety, and realized that something had disturbed His disciple. Easily reading Peter's thoughts, He placed His finger on the cause of the trouble. " What thinkest thou, Simon? of whom do the kings of earth take custom or tribute? of their own children or of strangers? Peter saith unto him, Of strangers. Jesus saith unto him, Then are the children free " (vv. 24-26).

The Fish with a Coin in its Mouth

" Notwithstanding, lest we should offend them, go thou to the sea, and cast an hook, and take up the fish that first cometh up; and when thou hast opened his mouth, thou shalt find a piece of money: that take, and give unto them for me and thee " (v. 27). Peter went to obey his Master, and it was a strange experience when he saw the fulfilment of Christ's prediction. Certain critics have ridiculed the account; yet missionaries from the Holy Land assure us that there was no miracle whatsoever in the fact that the fish had a coin in its mouth. A certain type of fish found in the sea of Galilee carries its young in its mouth, and when these are old enough to begin their separate existence, the parent fish will replace them with a stone or any other suitable object. Even today, fishermen from Galilee can shew coins which they have taken from the mouths of such fish. Nevertheless there was a two-fold miracle in Peter's exploit. The Lord knew that the coin would be in the mouth of the *first* fish to be caught; and secondly, He knew its value, and said it would be sufficient to pay for both Peter and Himself. " That take and give them *for me and thee.*"

The Christ with a Charm in His Message

Christ had wonderful ways of imparting truth. (i) *How great His claim.* If the princes of a royal household are exempt from the taxation demanded by their father, then the Prince of Heaven could not be expected to do as had been suggested. (ii) *How great His concern.* ". . . lest we should offend them." He knew that if men's hearts were biased against Him, their ears would be closed to His message. He was keen not to erect intellectual barriers which might hinder the proclamation of the Gospel. (iii) *How great His care.* ". . . for me and thee."* We shall never know how many times the Lord met the need of His followers. Yet, here at least is another example of His great kindness. When He paid Peter's debt and delivered him from the requirements of the law, He surely taught, in principle, that in like manner He would soon pay Peter's eternal debt. Christ the Son of God had deliberately chosen to be one with Peter in responsibility, that Peter might become one with Him in freedom. ". . . *for me and thee.*"

THE HUSBANDMAN . . . who paid strange wages

(MATTHEW 20:9)

You are a most interesting character, Mr. Unknown Husbandman, and your delightful ways have caused a great amount of discussion. A man whose actions are unpredictable is always a source of interest, but you succeeded in surprising a world. Many of us would have liked to accompany you that morning when you went into the market place in search of labourers. Your first employees were sent into the vineyards at 6 a.m. After you had eaten your breakfast, you visited the workmen and decided that it had become necessary to employ more hands. These commenced their belated shift at 9 a.m. This unusual procedure was repeated at 12 noon, and again at 3 p.m. Your method of seeking workmen seems totally foreign to western ways, and we have often wondered why you did not save time and trouble by hiring sufficient men when you first visited the market place. Yet at 5 p.m. you asked others to go and work for one hour, and at the end of the day these received a full day's wages. In the attempt to explain this unexpected generosity, we have asked several questions. Mr. Husbandman, we wish you were here to answer them.

Why hire so few men at 6 a.m.?

We rejected the idea that you were mean, and expected a few men to do the work of many. Your magnificent gesture toward the last batch of men outlaws any suggestion of meanness. We also asked if you were inexperienced in assessing the number of men required for the completion of the task. The successive hirings denote that had such been the case, you were very slow at learning your trade. When a business man has to be taught the same lesson four times in one day, there is obviously something wrong with his business. We decided, therefore, that the fault was in the workmen. They had a go-slow policy in order to lengthen the time of their employment. And since you were anxious to get the job finished on that particular day, it became necessary to increase the number of your workmen. The later arrivals worked well for a time, but were eventually influenced by their leaders. Dear friend, weren't you disgusted with them?

Why did the five o'clock men wait so long?

It was a very trying experience to wait eleven hours in a market place. As the day began to pass away and the shadows of night gathered, common sense would suggest a homegoing with a promise to return early the following morning. It must have seemed most unlikely that a man would engage labour at such a late hour; yet these would-be employees continued their weary vigil. Husbandman, were they desperate? Were they anxious to obtain food for their families? Were their prayers answered when you appeared on the scene? How we would love to obtain your answers to all these thought-provoking questions! Yet one thing needs no explanation. These men worked conscientiously when they entered into your vineyard. They put their best endeavours into the task, and while they could not equal the number of baskets filled by the men who had slowly worked for twelve hours, they at least did their best.

Why did you pay them a full day's wages?

Obviously you were very pleased with their efforts. They had fewer boxes of grapes to place at your feet, but they had more perspiration on their brows. It seems to us that you were more concerned with the way they had worked than with the results achieved. They had done their utmost at the job, and you revealed your appreciation in the magnificent wages which left them speechless with surprise. Mr. Husbandman, we heard about you because Jesus of Nazareth introduced you as the theme of one of His outstanding sermons. When thinking of eternal rewards, Simon Peter said, " Behold, we have forsaken all, and followed thee; what shall we have therefore? And Jesus said . . . And every one that hath forsaken houses, or brethren, or sisters, or father, or mother . . . for my name's sake, shall receive a hundredfold, and shall inherit everlasting life " (Matt. 19:27-29). It seems quite clear to us now that the Lord Jesus realized He would have many followers who would prove to be half-hearted and unenthusiastic. He therefore desired to teach that, when He returns at the end of life's day to reward His servants, His awards will be given not to those people expecting them, but to the faithful people who did their utmost in His service.

THE GUEST . . . who refused a wedding garment

(MATTHEW 22:12)

When the Lord Jesus spoke about the king who made a marriage for his son, He gave to the world one of His most comprehensive parables. The far-reaching implications of this message went beyond the immediate circumstances of His day, and embraced the entire age of grace. In speaking of the people who openly spurned the invitation to the wedding, Christ undoubtedly referred to the Jewish rejection of God's proffered grace. Yet out of this tragedy came a greater invitation to a wider audience. "Then saith he to his servants, The wedding is ready . . . Go ye therefore into the highways, and as many as ye shall find, bid to the marriage. So those servants went out into the highways, and gathered together all as many as they found, both bad and good: and the wedding was furnished with guests" (Matt. 22:9,10).

The Glad Request

It is significant that class distinction was unknown in this great message. The earlier invitation to the privileged few had been superseded by a far greater declaration — "Whosoever will may come." The "casting away of them" resulted in "the reconciling of the world" (Rom. 11:15). Thus the servants of the great king went out in every direction to seek guests for the wedding, and probably the scenes which took place beggared description. It seemed a fantasy that a king should welcome tramps to his palace. Yet the messengers of the royal household assured every one that this was the king's intention. It was indeed a great request, and nothing else could so adequately describe the wonder of the Gospel message. God is determined to honour His Son, and sinners of all nations are invited to the marriage supper of the Lamb.

The Glorious Raiment

An eastern wedding was always a most colourful affair, but a royal wedding was a scene of brilliant magnificence. Every guest was clothed in special garments provided by the king, and the entire scene became one of unprecedented splendour. The cost of supplying this raiment was very great, but no expense was ever spared in the matter of honouring a king's son. Bought at great price, the garments were offered free to all the guests. Therefore when the servants brought the poor, the wretched, the filthy, and the unlovely to the wedding, the colourful garments offered by the attendant seemed in strange contrast to the rags of the people. A quick wash to remove dirt, a putting off of rags, and a glad acceptance of the offered garment, were sufficient to turn a beggar into a prince. Probably this was the Saviour's best illustration of the garments of salvation. Provided at the greatest cost, they are offered free to sinners. We put away the rags of our self-righteousness, and reaching forth the hand of faith, we accept the garments of grace and stand clothed in the righteousness of Christ. Glorious raiment indeed!

The Great Refusal

"And when the king came in to see the guests, he saw there a man which had not on a wedding garment: and he saith unto him, Friend, how camest thou in hither not having a wedding garment? And he was speechless " (vv. 11, 12). The king was perfectly justified in asking the question, for he had made ample provision to meet the needs of all his guests. Surely, this particular guest could not have been clad in rags, or he would have readily seized the chance to hide his poverty. Perhaps his garments were new, and he was proud of them. He was not like the other guests. Maybe he was a Pharisee and said, "I am not as other men are . . . or even as these publicans." He therefore refused the offer of the garment, believing that he was perfectly presentable for the king's banquet.

The Ghastly Result

" Then said the king to the servants, Bind him hand and foot, and take him away, and cast him into outer darkness; there shall be weeping and gnashing of teeth " (v. 13). An expression of penitence at that late hour would be totally unacceptable. The silly man had refused a king's offer. He had done so deliberately, and had thereby insulted a king's grace and dishonoured a king's son. He was exceedingly guilty, and was responsible for his own misfortune. This was a tragedy which might easily have been avoided.

"Who hath ears to hear, let him hear."

THE DIVINE PREACHER . . . and His greatest sermon

(MATTHEW 27:45-52)

The Lord Jesus Christ was a man of supreme confidence, who was never surprised into rash action, and walked calmly along the path of His Father's will. When the crowd endeavoured to push Him over the brow of a hill, He passed through their midst and no one could hurt Him. When Peter would have attacked the enemies in the garden of Gethsemane, the Lord told him to put away his sword, for had it been necessary twelve legions of angels could have been summoned to His assistance. Yet of all such instances found in the New Testament the greatest is one of the lesser known. One day when critics and unbelievers refused to accept His authority, Jesus said, " When ye have lifted up the Son of man, then shall ye know that I am he . . . He that sent me is with me: the Father hath not left me alone . . . The Father that sent me beareth witness of me " (John 8:28-29; 8:18). The Lord Jesus fully realized that when His own voice would be unable to testify, the Father would bear witness of Him. And the way in which His prediction was fulfilled revealed the greatest truth. At the appointed time God preached His sermon—without words.

God witnessed to the purpose of the cross

It was nearly midday when the watching crowds at Calvary first became aware of the changes in the heavens. They had been intently gazing at the sufferers, and many had taunted Christ with their sneers and jeers. Then someone noticed the changing sky and expressed his amazement, for it seemed that the sun was dying. " Now from the sixth hour there was darkness over all the land unto the ninth hour." And God commenced His sermon! He could not have done a greater thing to witness to the purpose of the cross. Such an event had never taken place before, and has not happened since. The king of the celestial realm was blotted out by an accumulation of dark clouds brought together from all parts of the heavens. As fearful eyes watched the phenomenon, men wondered if the sun would ever be visible again. Then after three hours the welcome radiance filtered through the gloom, and it appeared as though a resurrection had taken place in the sky. God blotted out the sun in order to testify of the other miracle taking place on the cross. There the eternal Son was dying amid the darkness of a world's sin; yet the catastrophe was not to be for ever, for after three days He arose again, nevermore to die.

God witnessed to the path of the cross

"And, behold, the veil of the temple was rent in twain from the top to the bottom." Horrified priests stood appalled as the rending sound destroyed the silence of the sacred house. Unseen hands rudely tore the great veil, to reveal the mercy seat. Only the high priest had seen that sacred emblem, for on the day of atonement he alone was permitted to enter within the holiest place. Now everything had changed. Christ had died to open a new and a living way to the throne of grace, and the rending of the veil demonstrated the fact that what had been a private footpath walked by one privileged leader, had now become a highway along which all might approach the Father. It was not without significance that the break came from " the top to the bottom." Had it commenced on earth, priests might have seized the veil and brought it together again. The rending came from heaven and continued to the floor, so that even the smallest could have access to the place of communion.

God witnessed to the power of the cross

"And the graves were opened; and many bodies of the saints which slept arose, and came out of the graves after his resurrection, and went into the holy city and appeared unto many." Probably there were many sorrowful hearts in Jerusalem, where loved ones were sadly missed. Bereavement had removed the joy of homes, and families had been left to mourn. Then this miracle took place. The risen ones seemed to say, " Why do you weep? Dry your eyes, for we are not dead. The Lord has died for us, and through His triumph we live—absent from the body and at home with the Lord." In this extraordinary manner God completed His preaching. His wordless sermon provided the greatest message ever given in this world, and justified the confidence expressed in the prediction of the Saviour. It was heaven's testimony to the value of the death of Christ.

MR. TALKATIVE . . . whose words were somewhat jumbled (MARK 7:31-37)

One of the characters introduced by John Bunyan was Mr. Talkative, who joined Christian and Faithful on the road to the celestial city. He was an engaging personality, whose knowledge extended to all matters under the sun. He could quote Scripture or give tips for gamblers; he could chant hymns or utter blasphemies; he was a great talker, at home in any company. John Bunyan described how for a while Faithful was pleasantly surprised by the new companion, but finally Christian said, " This man is for any company and for any talk. As he talketh now with you, so will he talk when he is on the ale-bench, and the more drink he hath in his crown the more of these things he hath in his mouth. Faith hath no place in his heart, or house, or speech; all he hath lieth in his tongue, and his religion is to make a noise therewith." Maybe, Bunyan first found Talkative in Mark's Gospel!

The Strange Man

"And they bring unto Jesus one that was deaf, and had an impediment in his speech; and they beseech him to put his hand upon him " (Mark 7:32). This was one of the most remarkable cases ever brought to the Saviour. The man was deaf—it was not possible to speak directly to his soul. He was able to talk—but no one was able to understand what he said, for there was something wrong with his speech. And these disabilities were inextricably connected. The words of the great Teacher were unheard, and even the greatest of sermons left the man unmoved. Truth never reached his soul, for his ears were closed. He would never have come to Christ unless other people had brought him. His mumblings lacked intelligence. We must excuse John Mark for forgetting to add the man's name. He was Mr. Talkative, whose descendants are still with us. Are there not many people who can as readily converse about spiritual things as about worldly things? Can they not quote Scripture in support of their own unholy practices? Yet they immediately protest when their own personal need is suggested. They never hear the Master's word—they are deaf; they talk—but have an impediment in their speech.

The Special Methods

"And Jesus took him aside from the multitude, and put his fingers into his ears . . ." Slowly, firmly, the Saviour held the man's arm and resolutely led him away from the crowd. The people were still able to see from the distance, but the Saviour's action was sufficient to make Mr. Talkative realize that Jesus was interested in him personally. Then, as they turned to face each other, Christ placed His fingers into the deaf ears of the strange man, and a remarkable change came over the scene. Mr. Talkative ceased his incoherent mumblings, and became delightfully submissive. Opened ears cleared the way to his soul; he heard the message of Christ and responded. A willingness to co-operate came over his once difficult mind, and when Christ asked him to open his mouth, he obeyed the command, and was healed of the impediment which had confused all his utterances. Then, side by side, they returned to the crowd, who "were beyond measure astonished, saying, He hath done all things well: he maketh both the deaf to hear, and the dumb to speak" (v. 37).

The Suggestive Miracle

This is one of the outstanding miracles of the Lord. It is for that reason this man may be likened to John Bunyan's Mr. Talkative. It is a most difficult task to persuade certain people that they need the saving power of Christ. They are truly sincere when they recognize the need of other people, yet strangely blind in regard to their own predicament. It would appear that the salvation of such people depends upon the faithful intercession of their spiritual friends. *"And they bring unto him* one that was deaf and had an impediment in his speech." The power of Christ knows no limitations when He is assisted by the loyal co-operation of His disciples. If Mr. Talkative belongs to my own family I should find comfort in the fact that prayer can perform the impossible.

THE SAVIOUR . . . who disguised Himself

(MARK 16:12; LUKE 24)

The Emmaus story is among the best known of the Scriptures, but our familiarity with its details is apt to interfere with our understanding of its more serious teaching. Four questions are suggested by this stimulating account. (i) Why were the disciples going to Emmaus? It is worthy of note that apart from their contact with the Saviour, the journey was a waste of time. Their purpose in visiting Emmaus was unfulfilled, for they returned almost immediately. (ii) Why did they fail to recognize the Lord Jesus? (iii) Why did they enjoy the Stranger's sermon when its opening statements charged them with great folly? (iv) Why did they return at such a late hour of the night, and thus prove the inadvisability of their walk to Emmaus?

The Strange Road

Calvary had completely ruined the hopes of the disciples. These delightful people had followed Christ because they honestly believed He would establish the Messianic kingdom. Every day they witnessed new manifestations of power, and they never questioned the imminence of His coronation. When He surrendered to His enemies and was led forth to be nailed to a cross, their hearts turned to stone. Weary and despondent, they began making plans for the future, and ultimately two of the company decided to return home. Their walk into the country took them away from the cross; their backs were toward the sanctuary, and every step was one taken in the wrong direction. The Emmaus road has had many travellers, for embittered men have often made a contemporary Judas an excuse for backsliding. In the greater issues of life, the Emmaus road is a cul-de-sac and not a highway.

The Strange Redeemer

"And it came to pass, that, while they communed together and reasoned, Jesus himself drew near, and went with them. But their eyes were holden that they should not know him " (Luke 24:15-16). Had Christ revealed Himself immediately, and commanded their return to Jerusalem, they would have obeyed instantly; but their most intimate difficulties would have remained. There was very much more at stake than their return to the holy city. Recurring problems had ruined their peace of mind, and a strange unrest had conquered their hearts. In order to deal with these hidden troubles, the Lord Jesus disguised Himself and drew near. " He appeared in another form " (Mark 16:12). And thus He was able to handle the difficult task of revealing to two headstrong disciples the fact that they were capable of making mistakes.

The Strange Reaction

His sermon had an inauspicious beginning, and could never be a pattern for ministerial students. He began by calling His audience " fools." Yet in some mysterious fashion His message was delivered in a delightful way that made their hearts burn. We believe literature would have been enriched immeasurably had Christ's sermon been preserved for posterity. He systematically expounded in all the Scriptures the things concerning Himself, and His utterances cheered their drooping spirits. They had never heard such a message, for it proved that the cross would become the beacon from which radiant happiness would shine out to a world. They had been wrong in all their conclusions. The Lord Jesus touched the trouble-spot in their agitated souls; but without His disguise, this would have been impossible.

The Strange Return

When Christ accepted their invitation to supper, the scene was set for their greatest surprise. As He broke the bread, " they knew Him by the nail prints in His hands." Then their plans were instantly changed, as they desired to rejoin the brethren. The loneliness of the road, and the dangers of the night, were unable to keep them in Emmaus, for " they rose up the same hour and returned to Jerusalem." The darkness of their night of sorrow had given place to a dawn, and they desired to spend the new day in fellowship with the people of God. And as it was, so it is. Man is never so stupid as when he journeys away from the cross. A tent at Calvary is better than a palace in Emmaus.

THE SOLDIER . . . who conquered his
enemies without fighting

This Gentile soldier of a bygone age has won the admiration of the world. His restraint in face of provocation; his dignity in spite of insult and enmity; his forbearance and tolerance when open aggression might have been excusable, gained for him the respect of those whose land he had come to dominate. He was a man of outstanding quality.

Kindness Overcoming Hatred

Racial pride was a supreme characteristic in Israel, and patriotic Jews found it extremely difficult to beg from the Carpenter of Nazareth. The elders of the synagogues constantly urged their followers to boycott the meetings of Christ, and it was a startling sight when these same elders came to seek the Master's help. "And a certain centurion's servant, who was dear unto him, was sick, and ready to die. And when he heard of Jesus, *he sent unto him the elders of the Jews,* beseeching him that he would come and heal his servant. And when they came to Jesus, they besought him instantly, saying, That he was worthy for whom he should do this: for he loveth our nation, and he hath built us a synagogue." Their testimony gave eloquent evidence of the power of human kindness. All their bitter resentment and passionate opposition had been challenged and overcome by the kindliness of this Roman. The sunlight of his gracious personality had opened the flowers of appreciation which had been fast closed in their night of bitterness. They put aside their prejudice; swallowed their pride, and on behalf of their Gentile friend sought the help of the Saviour.

Humility Overcoming Pride

The man for whom they sought assistance was a centurion—a captain in Caesar's army of occupation. He was no ordinary man, and his qualities had been recognized by his superiors. His promotion to higher rank had not spoiled him, and when necessity arose, he was not above seeking the help of a humble Carpenter whose exploits had aroused the enmity of many of his friends.

Finally, he openly confessed his unworthiness of the approach of Christ, and said his home was no fit place for the Son of God. Humility is a flower which blooms in the garden of graciousness. In some climes it is very rare orchid.

Faith Overcoming Doubt

" Then Jesus went with them. And when he was now not far from the house, the centurion sent friends to him, saying unto him, Lord, trouble not thyself: for I am not worthy that thou shouldest enter under my roof . . . say in a word, and my servant shall be healed. For I also am a man set under authority, having under me soldiers, and I say unto one, Go, and he goeth; and to another, Come, and he cometh; and to my servant, Do this, and he doeth it." The officer saw Caesar's kingdom and recognized that the weight of his own commands was only explained by the authority he represented. He saw also a greater empire in which Jesus of Nazareth held high office. The Teacher represented eternal powers, and unseen angelic servants were waiting to fulfil His desires. " Speak the word only, and my servant shall be healed." Real faith sees the invisible; laughs at the impossible, and cries aloud in thanksgiving even before the deed is accomplished.

Grace Overcoming Need

" And they that were sent, returning to the house, found the servant whole that had been sick." It would appear from Matthew's account of the same story that as a last desperate measure, the captain himself had gone out to the roadway to voice his humble protest against the unworthiness of his own abode. Thus the Lord was able to say to him, " Go thy way; and as thou hast believed, so be it done unto thee. And his servant was healed in the selfsame hour " (Matt. 8:13). This ancient story is rich in truth. (i) The centurion was one of the best people of his day, yet he still had need of Christ. (ii) The grace of God as manifest in Christ was both able and willing to respond to the appeal for help. (iii) The Lord Jesus is " the same yesterday, and today, and forever." Therefore I can follow the example of the centurion, remembering that what might be lacking in my faith, will be more than supplied by the kindness of God.

JOANNA . . . the prime minister's wife who followed Jesus (Luke 8:3)

The Countess of Huntington was fond of quoting Paul's statement in 1 Corinthians 1:26-27, "For ye see your calling, brethren, how that not many wise men after the flesh. not many mighty, not many noble, are called . . ." The great lady quietly reminded her listeners that Paul said, "not *many* noble are called." Had Paul stated "not *any* noble are called," the countess would have been prevented from joining the ranks of the blessed. In all probability she would have welcomed an opportunity of speaking with Joanna, the wife of Herod's prime minister. These two ladies of highest society would have had much in common.

Her Deliverance by Christ

"And certain women, which had been healed of evil spirits and infirmities, Mary called Magdalene, out of whom went seven devils, and Joanna the wife of Chuza, Herod's steward, and Susanna, and many others, which ministered unto him of their substance . . ." (Luke 8:2-3). It is most suggestive that the name of this eminent woman is second on the list of lady disciples. It is not clear whether she had been delivered of evil spirits or healed of some infirmity, but we know that a great sense of need had brought her to the Saviour. Her position in society, and the prosperity which probably attended her station in life, guaranteed for her the best medical skill available in the land. Her elegant home had been visited by the king's own physicians, and no expense had been spared in the urgent quest of seeking relief from her complaint. Yet every attempt had failed, and finally this lady had been left with the unpleasant prospect of being ill for the rest of her life. And then she thought of Jesus of Nazareth. She came to Him, and "was healed of her infirmity."

Her Devotion to Christ

The true greatness of her soul was fully revealed in the events which followed that wonderful day. Her husband would naturally rejoice, but it is problematical whether he would be prepared for what was still to come. His master,

King Herod, was not kindly disposed toward the Nazarene, and the evil influences of court life would not be helpful to anyone whose interests were with the Saviour. Had Joanna been content to remain a respectable convert, or even to give liberal donations to the work of the Teacher, she would have had the support of all her friends. Yet when she ministered to Jesus; when she helped prepare meals, and did the mundane tasks of daily life, it seemed that she was disgracing her position. This was entirely beneath her station in life, and Herod would certainly express his keen displeasure. Joanna's actions could have easily been misunderstood, and her husband might have been critical of her constant attention on another man. Serenely, she followed her Lord, and her devotion increased in intensity daily.

Her Dependability for Christ

When it became evident that Jesus was to be sentenced to death, many of His followers left Him, and finally only a few were left to witness His death. "And the women also, which came with Him from Galilee, followed after, and beheld the sepulchre, and how His body was laid. And they returned and prepared spices and ointments; and rested the sabbath day according to the commandment. Now upon the first day of the week . . . they came unto the sepulchre . . . It was Mary Magdalene, and Joanna, and Mary the mother of James . . ." (Luke 23:55; 24:10). Against the depression of those dread days, the names of these devoted women shine as stars in a dark sky. Not even the disappointment occasioned by the cross had altered for one moment their intense loyalty to the Lord. Dependability is a great characteristic, but never is it seen to greater advantage than in the story of these brave women. Much of Joanna's account is hidden from us. We wonder whether or not her husband disowned her; whether her former friends scorned and ridiculed her; whether she was obliged to sacrifice everything in order to follow the dictates of her conscience. She became a princess in the royal household of heaven, and her name has been immortally inscribed among those whose love for Christ outshone all else in life.

THE WOMAN . . . who touched the hem of Christ's garment
(LUKE 8:43-44)

"And a woman having an issue of blood twelve years, which had spent all her living upon physicians, neither could be healed of any, came behind him, and touched the border of his garment: and immediately her issue of blood stanched." And in these few simple sentences, Dr. Luke recorded one of the most suggestive of all Christ's miracles. "A woman who had spent all her living upon physicians." Day after day, week after week, this worried soul had visited surgeries; time after time she had waited her turn, and had gone away with new hopes rising in her heart. But all her efforts had been in vain. This is the type of story with which John Bunyan would have revelled. He would have visited that woman in her home, and accompanied her as she went to see her physicians. He would have carefully noted the names of her doctors, and perhaps would have found them to be most suggestive. To him, quite obviously, this poor woman would have been the sinner seeking relief from inbred sin; the doctors would have been the physicians of the world, and the grand climax would have represented the moment when the soul bowed before Christ.

The Psychiatrist—Dr. Don't Worry

The Gospel of Christ always begets a sense of personal need, and in the desperate struggle which follows, the sinner has either to yield to the insistent pleadings of the Saviour, or seek elsewhere for the relief demanded by his harassed soul. A change of environment, a visit to fresh surroundings, a complete relaxation from the cares and strain of life, may work wonders in any patient, providing the cause of the trouble is not deep-seated. Many people stay away from religious meetings deciding that conviction is just a disease of the mind. They endeavour to cure it by excessive worldliness. The treatment is most expensive, particularly since it provides no cure.

The Dietician—Dr. Diet

This physician is very famous. His treatment promises permanent cure through elimination. His is the method of giving up things. The patient is urged to adhere strictly to diet, and through his complete denial of certain commodities, both body and soul are purified. In the spiritual realm, these doctors thrive. The sinner is urged to forsake every appearance of evil; to avoid anything detrimental to spiritual progress. He must shun the world and all its allurements; he is urged steadfastly to live the life of a recluse, and by the continuance of religious exercises will eventually attain that degree of spiritual health so urgently required. Immediate joy is unobtainable under this type of treatment, and the doctor is careful to explain that only those who endure to the end can ever hope to be saved.

The Specialist—Dr. Moderation

This is the wisest of all earth's physicians. With particular care he examines his patients, and outlines methods by which health may become a reality. A little of this and a little of that. Sufficient religion to satisfy the qualms of conscience; sufficient worldliness to please the innate longings of the flesh. The mountain-top for the fresh air and viewpoints of the eternal; the valley for the fellowship and delights of worldliness. Everything is all right in moderation. It would not be saying too much to add that every Christian has heard the voice of this eminent doctor. Perhaps John Bunyan would have visualised all these men, and would have underlined the text, *"A woman who had spent all her living upon physicians, neither could be healed of any."* The ancient sufferer " came behind Jesus, and touched the border of his garment: and immediately her issue of blood stanched . . . And Jesus said unto her, Daughter, be of good comfort: thy faith hath made thee whole; go in peace." And since Bunyan was also a preacher, he might have indicated that the story divided into three sections. (i) The trial of her faith. (ii) The touch of her faith. (iii) The triumph of her faith. It is a great thing to know a doctor whose reputation is equalled by his ability. Even the people of Palestine recognized this fact when they called Jesus " The Great Physician."

> Oh, touch the hem of His garment!
> And thou too shalt be free;
> His saving power, this very hour,
> Shall give new life to thee.

THE DISCIPLES . . . who had sleeping sickness
(Luke 9:32)

"But Peter and they that were with him were heavy with sleep: and when they were awake, they saw his glory. . . ." There are three instances of sleeping disciples mentioned in the New Testament, and in each case the time spent in slumber proved to be exceedingly costly. When the Lord Jesus led His faithful followers into the Mount of Transfiguration they did not realize what amazing events were about to take place. Determined to remain with Him during the night watches, they sat down on the ground and were soon asleep. That they awakened just in time to see a transfigured Lord, and then to accompany Him into the valley, seems to suggest that they had slept for most of the night. We shall never know how much they missed.

They Slept and Missed His Glory

"When they were awake, they saw his glory, and the two men that stood with him." Their brief vision left such an indelible impression upon their memories that even after thirty years the apostle Peter wrote, "We were with him in the holy mount" (2 Pet. 1:18). The disciples never forgot the soul-stirring vision of the face that shone as the sun, and the garments which were white and glistening. They remembered how God said, "This is my beloved Son: hear him." With awe and amazement they recalled how Moses and Elijah spake of the "decease which he should accomplish at Jerusalem," and probably speculated as to the reason why both the Law and the Prophets were so informed of the Messiah's death. The glory of that resplendent scene was indescribable. Radiance emanated from their beloved Master, and He seemed more like the King of angels than the hero of poor fishermen. All this happened just prior to the dawn, and we are obliged to ask what untold revelations might have been theirs had they remained awake and watchful. Perhaps their slumbers accounted for their subsequent defeat in the valley.

They Slept and Missed His Passion

There was a strange and eerie silence in the garden of Gethsemane on the night when Jesus was betrayed. The stillness preceding the breaking of the storm only accentuated the heartbreaks of the Lord Jesus. Fully conscious of His great need, He temporarily withdrew from the crowds and, accompanied by three disciples, "went, as he was wont, to the mount of Olives . . And being in an agony he prayed more earnestly: and his sweat was as it were great drops of blood falling down to the ground. And when he rose up from prayer, and was come to his disciples, he found them sleeping for sorrow" (Luke 22: 39-45). Indeed we are left with a question: If these men were sleeping, who witnessed the sufferings of Christ? Possibly one of the men who had been left outside the garden became a little impatient and came in search of his friends. If this happened, then he arrived in time to witness the indescribable. The love of God's heart was overflowing, and the streams of eternal compassion were reaching out to earth's remotest end. Yet if the disciples had remained awake during those moments of agonizing conflict, their appreciation of the price paid for our redemption might have increased immeasurably. Their sleep in the garden preceded the fear that made them forsake their Lord.

They Slept and Missed Eternal Joys

When the disciples asked for signs of the Lord's return, He described ten virgins going forth in anticipation of a wedding (Matt. 25:1-13). While the bridegroom tarried they all slumbered and slept, but when the cry went forth, "Behold, the bridegroom cometh," they immediately arose and went forth to meet him. Thereupon five foolish virgins became instantly conscious of their need, and while they vainly sought hurriedly to prepare for the future, their moment of opportunity passed by. The five wise virgins entered into the marriage, and had great joy in the presence of the bridegroom. Yet each one of the five should have been accompanied by a convert! The Lord Jesus cited this as an indication of conditions to exist in the world prior to His return. Souls would be perishing while Christendom remained inactive and sleepy. His word has been fulfilled. "Watch therefore, for in such an hour . . the Son of man cometh."

THE PLOUGHMAN . . . who had eyes in the back of his head

"And Jesus said . . . No man, having put his hand to the plough, and looking back, is fit for the kingdom of God." It is not without significance that this statement was made at the end of three interviews with the Saviour. Young men had been confronted by the challenge of discipleship, and apparently all three had missed the opportunity of following the Lord Jesus. This suggested to the Lord the picture of the half-hearted ploughman.

Discipleship Demands Resolution

"And it came to pass, that, as they went in the way, a certain man said unto him, Lord, I will follow thee whithersoever thou goest. And Jesus said unto him, Foxes have holes, and the birds of the air have nests. but the Son of man hath not where to lay his head." The silence that followed the announcement seemed ominous. Amid the prevailing excitement of a revival service, an impressionable soul spontaneously moved to respond to the call of Christ. It should be carefully noted that he came on his own initiative. Stirred to the depths of his heart, he hastened to pledge allegiance to the cause of the new Teacher. Christ's sombre warning was as the chilly blast of a mid-winter's wind. The fervour of the meetings had thrilled the young man, and he could not understand how the future could be any different from the present. The Lord Jesus knew that such a disciple would be useless unless he was prepared to endure hardness. The ploughman who sets out to plough a field must be prepared for difficult places. Stones, roots, and rough ground may soon be encountered, and any half-hearted attempt at such an enterprise will only damage the plough and spoil the job.

Discipleship Demands Readiness

"And Jesus said unto another, Follow me. But he said, Lord, suffer me first to go and bury my father." Not all men are alike. Some impulsively rush to offer service; others retire into seclusion, fearing that their talents are unequal to the demands of the new life. The former needs to be retarded; the latter must always be encouraged. This man's excuse only revealed his unfitness of soul. Had his father been dead, he himself would have been attending to the funeral arrangements. It was considered the duty of the firstborn to lay the father's body to rest. The call to follow Christ was secondary to that of waiting to bury his —perhaps—still healthy father. Thus, in one request, he demonstrated that as a ploughman or as a disciple, he would be useless. A farmer cannot plough a field at any time. The state of the soil, and the weather, dictate the time for ploughing; and the wise farmer hurries to the task when the time is opportune. These things are also true in regard to discipleship. There are occasions when the cares of this world bog the spirit; there are days when our hearts are hard. God is best able to decide when His Spirit can work successfully, and every wise man will be ready to answer His call immediately it is heard. In farming or discipleship it is never safe to put off until tomorrow what should be done today.

Discipleship Demands Resignation

Probably greatly stirred by the refusal of the second man, another hastened to say, "Lord, I will follow thee; but let me first go bid them farewell, which are at home at my house." And Jesus, realizing the dangers of such a procedure, replied, "No man, having put his hand to the plough, and looking back, is fit for the kingdom of God." And if any casual reader should consider this attitude to be severe, let it be remembered that Jesus Himself loved to visit the homes of His followers. Such an answer is a sure guarantee that, had the man returned home, his family would have argued him out of his proposals. How can any man take up his cross and follow Christ if, all the while, the eyes in the back of his head are hungrily searching for the alluring pleasures left behind in a home, a business, or in some other place? Following Christ demands resignation—deliberate, sacrificial resignation. The successful disciple is the one who says, "I must be a Christian, or die." Every ploughman worthy of the name will recognize conditions suited to his enterprise, and will stay at his plough until his task is completed. And in like manner, should a soul be moved to exclaim, "Lord, I will follow thee whithersoever thou goest," then nothing should ever be permitted to prevent the fulfilment of that vow.

THE TRAVELLER . . . who fell among thieves

(LUKE 10:30)

"A certain man went down from Jerusalem to Jericho, and fell among thieves, which stripped him of his raiment, and wounded him, and departed, leaving him half dead " —and, as Dr. Parker once said, " He asked for it! " It is not possible for any man to turn his back upon the house of God and to walk toward Jericho—the city of the curse —and not to fall among thieves. The Bible has several examples of such foolish travellers.

The Ephesian Elder who lost his first love

There are travellers who set out with a fixed purpose of reaching a desired destination; there are others who stroll along aimlessly. Probably the man of Ephesus belonged to the latter class. Perfectly satisfied with the abundance of church services, and a little conceited over the obvious superiority of his church connections, the revered saint sauntered along without a care; and while he walked in his sleep, the evil thieves stole his greatest jewel. The Lord Jesus said of such a man, and the Church he represented, " I know thy works, and thy labour, and thy patience, and how thou canst not bear them which are evil . . . Nevertheless I have somewhat against thee, because thou hast left thy first love " (Rev. 2:2-4). If love warms the heart and cheers the assembly, then the Church at Ephesus had no heating apparatus.

The Psalmist who lost the joy of his salvation

King David was one of those unfortunate men whose eyes were permitted to rest for too long a time upon prohibited pleasures. His vision kindled an unholy fire upon the altar of his heart, and in those fires he sacrificed his peace of mind. The sordid story of murder reveals David walking away from the sanctuary. He had forgotten his former vows, and sought attractions on the road to Jericho. And then came the thugs! When the soul of David struggled back to consciousness, he discovered that serious harm had befallen his spiritual raiment. He had been stripped, and left naked in his guilt before God. The accusing eyes of the prophet were focused upon him, and the unwavering finger pointing at his heart added emphasis to the accusation, " Thou art the man." Broken-hearted, David bowed in despair, and discovered that the Jericho thieves had stolen his fairest treasure. Psalm 51 tells how he prayed, " Restore unto me the joy of thy salvation." Poor David, he should have known better.

The Prodigal who lost his father's fellowship

As he whistled his way along the road which led to the far country, the prodigal smiled. Bah! His father was old-fashioned and stodgy. The home was too circumscribed. He had left it forever. Ahead lay the far country and a grand time. Instinctively he lengthened his stride. The road was hazy. Visibility was never very good in the Jericho area, and some of the fog entered the mind of the boy. He was unable to recognize his own stupidity; he could not see what awaited him in the glamorous city, and he was too short-sighted to discern the base hypocrisy of the thieves who posed as friends. He fell among thieves who left him bewildered and penniless in a pig sty. When the disillusioned fellow began taking stock of his position, he discovered he had lost many treasures, including the fellowship of his father. In comparison with that tragedy, the loss of his money seemed insignificant.

The Crown of Life—the greatest jewel of all

"And to the angel of the church in Philadelphia write . . . Because thou hast kept the word of my patience, I also will keep thee from the hour of temptation. . . . Behold, I come quickly: hold that fast which thou hast, that no man take thy crown " (Rev. 3:7-11). This constitutes the greatest warning given to the Church, and to all who ever worked in the Church. No man can afford to lose his eternal crown of life, and the undivided attention of every individual should be devoted to the guarding of this great treasure. Jericho has never been a health resort, and the man of old should be a warning to all travellers.

JUDAS . . . who gambled and lost his soul
(LUKE 22:3-5)

The account of the treachery of Judas Iscariot is the most tragic story in history. It is beyond comprehension that a man who had occupied a position of trust and friendship in the disciple band, should ultimately betray his leader. Many questions have been asked concerning this pathetic episode; but one thing has become evident. It is that the complete story of Judas is summed up in the opening statement of Luke 22:4, "And he went *his* way." It is indeed most doubtful whether he ever went Christ's way.

The Way of Glory

"And Jesus ordained twelve, that they should be with him, and that he might send them forth to preach. Simon . . . James . . . and Judas Iscariot " (Mark 3:14-19). The foreknowledge of God does not alter the responsibility of man. Even although Christ knew what would take place, Judas of his own volition deliberately betrayed the Master. To him the call of Christ had been irresistible. It opened vistas of unprecedented possibilities. If this new leader were to be the Messiah, then the kingdom was at hand, and every man in the nation would have welcomed a place at the side of his King. Eagerly anticipating the splendour of a glorious future, Judas left his friends and followed the Saviour. And there is reason to believe that he worked as hard as anyone else in the days of preaching which followed. This was indeed *his own way,* and it is easy to imagine how fervently he proclaimed his message to all and sundry.

The Way of Greed

Many years later, when the apostle John described the criticisms made by Judas concerning Mary's gift of ointment, he wrote, " Then saith one of his disciples, Judas Iscariot, Simon's son, which should betray him, Why was not this ointment sold for three hundred pence, and given to the poor? This he said, not that he cared for the poor; but because he was a thief, and had the bag, and bare what was put therein " (John 12:4-6). There had been times when the disciples had been puzzled by the shortage of money. It was inconceivable that one of their number should steal from the common fund; and yet . . . ? Long afterward they remembered, and understood. "Judas went *his* way." It was the way of self-pleasing. Probably he argued with himself that his position as treasurer deserved remuneration. He therefore helped himself to money which was not his. Ultimately it was this love of gain which wrecked his soul. As the end of Christ's pilgrimage approached, Judas became increasingly suspicious that something had gone wrong. The promised kingdom seemed to be receding; the Master had grown sad and thoughtful; the enemies were becoming jubilant. Judas noted all these things, and realized that Christ's way and his own way were not parallel paths. When the Lord failed to take advantage of the delirious welcome afforded by the crowd as He rode into Jerusalem, Judas knew that tragedy loomed on the horizon.

The Way of Guilt

At an eastern feast, the offering of a sop by the host is recognized as a mark of favour. Almost the last thing Jesus did for Judas was to offer friendship. Judas replied with the traitor-kiss. When the betrayer felt the coins in his hand, he smiled. They were better than nothing! Yes, he was getting out while he was able! He went *his own way*. Poor man! With remorse playing havoc with his conscience; with his coins rudely scattered over the floor; with his hopes and plans completely broken, a poor tormented man, he went out to commit suicide. And of his final destiny there can be no doubt. Jesus prayed and said, ". . . those that thou gavest me I have kept, and none of them is lost, but the son of perdition; that the scripture might be fulfilled " (John 17:12). Certain eminent teachers have declared that Judas was Satan's imitation of the Son of God. They have drawn attention to the fact that the same title—" The son of perdition " is also used of the antichrist (2 Thess. 2:3). Mention has also been made of the fact that of Judas alone it is said ". . . from which Judas by transgression fell, that *he might go to his own place*" (Acts 1:25). Here are great mysteries; but one thing is certainly clear. Judas had staked his all; he was a reckless gambler. He lost because he had not the ability to see God's way was better than his own.

THE GARDEN CONFLICT . . . the world's greatest battle

The life of the Lord Jesus was a time of constant watchfulness against the wiles of Satan. One mistake would have been sufficient to wreck the entire plan of God's salvation; and both Christ and His enemy knew it. Through direct methods, when Jesus was promised the kingdoms of the world; and through indirect methods, when the spite and bitterness of men endeavoured to irritate and annoy Him, Satan continually tried to overcome the Son of God. " He was in all points tempted like as we are, yet without sin " (Heb. 4:15). And the nearer Christ went to His cross and victory, the more desperate became the enemy. It would appear that Satan finally abandoned any attempt to make Christ fall into sin, realizing that in this matter the Lord Jesus was invincible. There remained but one possibility. The garden of Gethsemane became the scene of the world's greatest conflict, when Satan tried to kill the Saviour before the triumph of the cross could be won.

The Great Conflict. How Great Christ's Subservience to the Will of God

"And he was withdrawn from them about a stone's cast, and kneeled down, and prayed, saying, Father, if thou be willing, remove this cup from me: nevertheless not my will, but thine, be done." There is reason to believe that this was Christ's greatest prayer. The writer to the Hebrews adds a few poignant details: " Who in the days of his flesh, when he had offered up prayers and supplications with strong crying and tears *unto him that was able to save him from death,* and was heard in that he feared " (Heb. 5:7). Obviously Christ dreaded death; but that could not have been the death of the cross. Calvary, and what lay beyond, brought great joy to the Lord's heart, for we read in Hebrews 12:2, ". . . *who for the joy that was set before him* endured the cross, despising the shame, and is set down at the right hand of the throne of God." The death dreaded by the Saviour was the premature death planned by the evil one. If Jesus had died in the garden of Gethsemane, the triumph of the cross would have been unknown. Therefore Satan directed against the physical resistance of the Lord Jesus every power at his command. In His moments of agonizing strain and weakness the Lord realized His need, and " the strong crying and tears " brought instant relief.

The Great Cry. How Great Christ's Supplication to the Heart of God

Language is inadequate to describe the spiritual stature of the Lord when, in spite of His intense longing to reach Calvary, He cried, " Not my will, but thine, be done." Yet it *was* the will of God to save Him, for the mind of the Son was in perfect alignment with the mind of the Father. Prayer was not a new exercise to the Lord Jesus. Day after day He had communed with God; yet these prayers in Gethsemane were unique. "And being in an agony he prayed *more earnestly*: and his sweat was as it were great drops of blood falling down to the ground." It would appear that this was a desperate cry for assistance. His life blood was being shed too soon. The appeal reached the heart of God, and the prayer was answered. "And there appeared an angel unto him from heaven, strengthening him " (Luke 22 : 43). This is probably the Bible's greatest portrait of prayer. If only the followers of Christ would emulate their Master's example, revival would begin immediately.

The Great Conquest. How Great Christ's Succour Through the Help of God

True prayer is always answered; but if we ask according to the will of God, the answer is always in the affirmative. The coming of the angel provided Christ with the much needed strength which enabled Him to overcome the fierce assault of Satan, and ultimately to proceed triumphantly to His cross. Satan's last great attempt to frustrate the purposes of God in Christ failed completely. Exultantly Paul was able to write, " And having spoiled principalities and powers, he made a show over them openly, triumphing over them in it " (Col. 2 : 15). The foundation of Calvary's victory was laid in the prayers of Gethsemane. And in this remarkable fashion God would teach us that life's greatest achievements are only made possible as we seek the place of prayer. A man is never so great as when he kneels before his Maker.

CALVARY . . . the world's greatest meeting place

Calvary stands in the centre of all the purposes of God; and it is fitting that around the cross men and women of all races should meet in unity of spirit. The Christ of the cross, and the cross of the Christ, represent the greatest meeting place in the world.

A Place of Revelation

With wonderment shining in their eyes, the centurion and the other people watched the Saviour, and marvelled at the things they witnessed. That He could ask His Father to forgive the apparently unpardonable crime, indicated virtue of high degree; and it was not a cause for amazement when the centurion suddenly exclaimed, " Truly this was the Son of God " (Matt. 27:54). No man can intelligently listen in the shadow of Calvary's cross and not increase his knowledge of the One who died there. The small green hill is a great vantage point from which to view the heart of God.

A Place of Supplication

" And the thief said unto Jesus, Lord, remember me when thou comest into thy kingdom " (Luke 23:42). It is highly improbable that this unfortunate man had ever had previous contacts with the Lord Jesus. His former habits had been characterized by vice, and his companions had been men of ill repute. Losing his grasp upon the finer things of life, he had drifted on tides of evil. Then in the closing moments of his life, he met the Saviour. They were fellow travellers on the road of sorrow. Indescribable charm emanated from the soul of Christ, and beneath its soothing power the criminal felt the pull of another world. His eyesight was remarkably good—he looked at the dying Jesus, and saw a King reigning in glory. He had never been so near to royalty, and he made splendid use of the occasion.

A Place of Meditation

" And sitting down, they watched him there " (Matt. 27:36). Amid the noisy clamour of that crowd of sensationalists who had come to stare at the executions, a company of men sat down patiently to watch the suffering prophet. They were anxious to see every detail of His agony and sufferings, and probably long afterward they were able to recount all the events of that fateful afternoon. Yet the greatest vision of that day could not be seen by mortal eyes. In that holy place of meditation many have since sat down to think, and during the course of their contemplations they have discovered the hill called Calvary to be a Jacob's ladder—a means of ascending into heaven.

A Place of Co-operation

" Now there stood by the cross of Jesus His mother . . . When Jesus therefore saw His mother, and the disciple standing by, whom He loved, He saith unto His mother, Woman, behold Thy son! Then saith He to the disciple, Behold Thy mother! And from that hour that disciple took her into his own home " (John 19:25-27). John was more privileged than all the other disciples, for into his faithful care the Lord Jesus entrusted His greatest earthly treasure. The disciple was commissioned to take his Lord's place in the life of the sorrowing Mary. The privilege carried heavy responsibilities, for not every disciple would be sufficiently trustworthy for this great task. The Lord knew John would not fail Him; and His mother, dearest and best of all earthly friends, would be safe in the care of the beloved apostle. Would my standard of loyalty beget such confidence?

A Place of Adoration

" And they sung a new song, saying, Thou art worthy . . . for thou wast slain, and hast redeemed us to God by Thy blood out of every kindred, and people, and tongue, and nation " (Rev. 5:9). When we reach heaven, many of our former experiences will undoubtedly have been forgotten; yet the cross will remain in our thoughts for ever. " We shall know our Redeemer when we reach the other side—we shall know Him by the nail prints in His hands." We shall realize also that our debt of love will never be repaid, and perhaps in the language of John Bunyan we shall say,

Blest Cross! Blest Sepulchre! Blest rather be
The Man who there was put to shame for me.

THE FIRST CHRISTMAS . . . the world's greatest miracle

(JOHN 1:14)

Many writers, ancient and modern, have written concerning the birth of Christ; but of them all, three stand out in bold relief. When Dr. Luke wrote his Gospel, he quoted the angels as saying, " For unto you is born this day in the city of David, a Saviour, which is Christ the Lord " (Luke 2:11). When Paul the theologian expressed the mind of the Church, he wrote ". . . great is the mystery of godliness: God was manifest in the flesh . . ." (1 Tim. 3:16). And finally, the apostle John said, " In the beginning was the Word, and the Word was with God, and the Word was God . . . And the Word was made flesh, and dwelt among us . . ." We would add to the words of the journalist, and say that this was the greatest event in history.

PROPOSITION 1. *If it be true that God came down to earth, surely His reasons for doing so were very great*

History teaches that in every crisis in human experience, God has been able to produce either man or angel capable of meeting the need. The judges and the prophets of ancient times all witness to this truth. Yet behind the Bethlehem incident is the greatest drama of all time. God was confronted by something which necessitated His own intervention. Neither man nor angel was equal to the demands of the moment, and thus God found it necessary to come down to earth. " The Word was made flesh." That compelling need—whatever it was—must have been exceedingly great, and we are obliged to discover its origin. Let the Scriptures supply the answer. " This is a faithful saying, and worthy of all acceptation, that Christ Jesus came into the world to save sinners " (1 Tim. 1:15). It was the need of man which brought the Almighty to earth; and in view of all that has already been said, we are now able to extend proposition one. If the story be true, then how great was the need of man.

PROPOSITION 2. *If it be true that God came down to earth, how great was His love*

It must never be forgotten that God saw the end from the beginning; and He who came to Bethlehem, came knowing that the road would lead on to Calvary. Yet in spite of the unprecedented anguish through which He would be called to pass, He turned not back. Fully realizing all that would be demanded of Him, He came into the world to save sinners. This great love was manifest in every miracle He performed, in every sermon delivered, and in every contact which He had with mankind. The same hands which upheld and controlled a world, were capable of lifting a little child to His knee. The same mind which conceived the songs of the birds was also interested in bringing songs to the hearts of needy people. He touched the untouchable lepers; He loved the unlovely demoniacs; He died for the ungrateful ungodly. There was love in all His words and deeds, and that love not only brought Him to a manger—it took Him to Calvary.

PROPOSITION 3. *If it be true that God came down to earth, then how great is man's opportunity*

A possible objection might be that this would be true for the people living in His day, but for us who are removed by twenty centuries from the time of His sojourn on earth, the proposition would not be strictly accurate. If we could sit at His feet, or even draw near to His side, then our opportunities would be measureless. Alas, we were born too late! These arguments seem convincing until we pause to remember that if God really came to earth, then His words would be utterly reliable. The incarnate Word said at a later date, " It is expedient for you that I go away: for if I go not away, the Comforter will not come unto you . . ." (John 16:7). Imprisoned within a body, the eternal spirit of Christ could not be in two places at once. Yet, in the Person of the returning Comforter, He could be everywhere at the same moment. Thus He was able to command His disciples, " Go ye into all the world and preach the Gospel." " And lo, *I am with you alway*" (Mark 16:15; Matt. 28:20). The Incarnate Word is now the Omnipresent Christ.

> O holy Child of Bethlehem,
>   Descend to us, we pray;
> Cast out our sin, and enter in
>   Be born in us today.
> We hear the Christmas angels
>   The great glad tidings tell:
> Oh, come to us, abide with us,
>   Our Lord Emmanuel.

SPRING-CLEANING . . . in the house of God

The cleansing of the temple was undoubtedly the realization of an ambition of Jesus. His Father's house had become a den of thieves, and was one of the most disappointing sights in the city. The rows of tables behind which sat the evil moneychangers; their constant endeavours to swindle foreign visitors by giving an exceedingly low rate of exchange for their currency; the stable-like courtyards where the tethered offerings constituted another source of robbery; all added to the horror of the place. The Lord could not interfere until " His hour had come," but immediately He had commenced His public ministry, He made His way to the temple to see again the people who marred the sanctity of God's house. Then stooping to lift some cords, he dexterously made a whip and with purposeful strides advanced on the moneychangers. Surely this was an inauspicious beginning to His ministry; but nothing could have been more prophetic in character.

The Cleansing Which Suggested Conversion

" And the Jews' passover was at hand, and Jesus went up to Jerusalem, and found in the temple those that sold oxen and sheep and doves, and the changers of money sitting: and when he had made a scourge of small cords, he drove them all out of the temple, and the sheep, and the oxen; and poured out the changers' money, and overthrew the tables; and said unto them that sold doves, Take these things hence; make not my Father's house an house of merchandise." His action clearly demonstrated His desire to restore sanctity to the house of God. It also leaves us with a very important question. What is the true temple of God? The Old Testament Scriptures reveal God's desire to live with His people. It would appear that Adam was created to meet a need in the divine heart. God desired fellowship, and it was not surprising when He came down in the cool of the evening to walk and talk with man. God's plans were hindered when sin defiled man's soul; but the Tabernacle in the wilderness, and Solomon's Temple, emphasized what had been already revealed. Human hearts were far more important than any building, and ultimately Paul was able to say, " Know ye not that *ye are the temple of God* " (1 Cor. 3 : 16). The defilement of the temple was indicative of the tragedy of the soul. Sin had entered both places, and the action of the Saviour indicated that true conversion takes place only when He is able to cleanse away the filth of the soul, and to fill the house with the sense of His presence.

The Cleansing Which Suggested Restoration.

After the initial cleansing of the temple, calm reigned supreme within the sacred house. Sin had been expelled, and in its place a simple dignity suggested that the Lord had returned to His house. The weeks passed by, and then a wizened old moneychanger suddenly appeared at the door, and after a moment's hesitation, set up his table. The priests permitted his return to business, and as the news spread through the city, all his colleagues returned to their places. When the animals were brought back, " the last state of that house was worse than the first." The ancient picture seems to be very modern. Many people whose hearts were once made clean by the Saviour, have permitted the return of the old sins. Their backslidden state can always be traced to their compromise, when the evil moneychangers first reappeared on the threshold of their inmost being. Once Satan gains a foothold in the life of a Christian, it becomes increasingly difficult to expel him. Compromise leads to defeat; and there is no more disappointing sight than that of a backslidden believer. Then Jesus came again to Jerusalem. " And Jesus went into the temple of God, and cast out all them that sold and bought in the temple, and overthrew the tables of the moneychangers, and the seats of them that sold doves . . . And the blind and the lame came to Him in the temple; and He healed them " (Matt. 21 : 12-14). And thus Christ cleansed the temple the second time. God said, " Return unto me . . . and I will heal thy backsliding." Nothing is too difficult for the Saviour when the hearts of His people are true sanctuaries. We may confidently expect healing when nothing of evil has been permitted to linger within the temple of God.

THE POOL OF BETHESDA . . . the pulpit
where angels preached (John 5:6)

It was the sabbath day in Jerusalem, and many people had neglected going to church. Bethesda, the sheep market pool, was a scene of lazy indolence, and on the steps surrounding its placid waters, the sick lay in frustrated expectancy. The synagogue service had ended, and some of the worshippers were walking toward the famous place. They passed beneath the arches made by the five porches, and saw before them " a great multitude of impotent folk, of blind, halt, withered, waiting for the moving of the water. For an angel went down at a certain season into the pool, and troubled the water: whosoever then first after the troubling of the water stepped in was made whole of whatsoever disease he had." Alas, on that sabbath day the waters were very still!

The Pool That Said God Still Lived

A great deal of discussion has taken place concerning the accuracy of this story. It has been said that the district was rich in medicinal qualities, and that periodic eruptions in the earth's strata filled the pool with healing propensities. Theologians have said the incidents always took place during such disturbances, and that every miracle was due to a man's being able to seize his opportunity when subterranean movements liberated elements beneficial to sick people. This, however, appears to be absurd. Either the account is true or it is not. None of these teachers explained why the healing powers were all exhausted after the first miracle, nor for that matter how, irrespective of the type of disease to be treated, the swirling waters always healed the seeking sufferer. The Bethesda pool was God's pulpit! Malachi had been the last of the prophets, and his ministry had almost been forgotten. The nation possessed a dead formalism, an ornate temple, but no prophet. Yet as long as the pool offered healing to sick souls, it did the work of the temple pulpit. The priestly theologians only spoke of healing; the pool supplied it. Perhaps that was the chief reason why folk were sitting around the still waters when they might have been in church.

The Power That Said God Still Listened

If the priests had known how to pray as did the people at the pool, there would have been no need for an angel to stir any waters. The need of a world is generally governed by the spirituality of the house of God. Every true sanctuary liberates more healing power than the sheep market pools of the world ever possessed. A dead church sends seekers elsewhere. The hopes and prayers of Israel had been transferred from the temple to the pool. When the waters were suddenly stirred; when wild confusion sent scores of unfortunates tumbling one over the other in a frantic bid to be first into the water; when someone emerged to cry aloud for joy, everyone realized that once again God had been sufficiently interested in His creatures to ordain another case of healing. Thus God tried to teach His people to be ready to respond whenever He should shew His hand.

The Preacher That Said God Still Loved

"And a certain man was there, which had an infirmity thirty and eight years. When Jesus saw him lie, and knew that he had been now a long time in that case, he saith unto him, Wilt thou be made whole?" There was no fuss, and the conversation was carried on in normal tones. "Sir," replied the sufferer, "I have no man when the water is troubled to put me into the pool: but while I am coming another steppeth down before me. Jesus saith unto him, Rise, take up thy bed, and walk. And immediately the man was made whole, and took up his bed, and walked: and on the same day was the sabbath." And the proud pharisaical people immediately misunderstood his motives, and accused him of forgetting the sanctity of God's day. And while they were arguing over the do's and don'ts of the law, the great Healer quietly withdrew. Yet He left behind a sermon without a text. It was the will of God that every man should have a chance of salvation, and since this lonely sufferer had none to help him, the love of God brought healing to his bedside. "Afterward Jesus findeth him in the temple." It is noteworthy that the man found his way into the sanctuary. God only visited the pool—He lived at the mercy seat!

THE SAVIOUR . . . and the reasons for His tears

(JOHN 11:35)

The shortest verse in the Bible is probably one of the greatest. Every student of the Bible appreciates the wonder of the miracles, yet it is problematical whether any super-natural display of healing power could ever present a greater sight than that of tears on the Lord's cheeks. It surpasses understanding that the King of angels should weep, and it is almost incomprehensible that He who had known eternal splendour should become acquainted with the heartbreaks of sinful men. There are three instances of such weeping recorded in the Scriptures, and a study of these texts reveals progression of thought.

He Wept Because Sin had Hurt the World

The death of Lazarus brought great grief to his sorrowing sisters, and it is easy for us to appreciate the poignancy of the scene described in John 11:33, "When Jesus saw Mary weeping, and the Jews also weeping which came with her, he groaned in the spirit, and was troubled." And within a few moments the watching crowd saw that "Jesus wept." Some of the greatest thinkers of the Church have advanced reasons for this expression of divine grief. (i) *He wept in sympathy for His friends.* Yet this reason can hardly be acceptable, for why should Christ weep in sympathy when He knew that Lazarus would soon be restored to his sisters? (ii) *He wept because He was about to bring Lazarus back into a world of sin.* It is also difficult to accept this explanation, for the Saviour had already said that this event would bring glory to His Father. (iii) *He wept because of the irreparable suffering which had been brought to God's fair world.* Many graves would be in the vicinity of the tomb of Lazarus, and Christ knew that behind each burial-place was a tale of woe. Disease and death had appeared to mar man's joy, and the scene around Christ was anything but what God had intended. Sin had hurt the world, and the contemplation of the tragedy hurt the Saviour. He wept.

He Wept Because Sin Was About to Hurt His People

"And when He was come near, He beheld the city, and wept over it, saying, If thou hadst known, even thou, at least in this thy day, the things which belong unto thy peace! but now they are hid from thine eyes. For the days shall come upon thee, that thine enemies shall cast a trench about thee, and compass thee round . . . and shall lay thee even with the ground . . . because thou knewest not the time of thy visitation " (Luke 19:41-44). When the Lord Jesus wept over the city of Jerusalem the crowds ceased their shouting " Hosanna to the Son of David," and as they slowly went away into the streets, the disappointed disciples realized they had lost their greatest opportunity of establishing the kingdom. The tears of their Master had banished thoughts of glory. He had wept because Israel's rejection of their Messiah would bring inescapable destruction to the city of David. The Lord knew all that would shortly take place, and the fact that their fate seemed to be thoroughly deserved could never take the pain from His heart. Had He been able to save the people, He would have done so; but, alas, there were certain things which even Christ could not do.

He Wept Because Sin was Beginning to Hurt Him

" Christ . . . who in the days of his flesh, when he had offered up prayers and supplications with strong crying and tears unto him who was able to save him from death, and was heard in that he feared " (Heb. 5:7). In describing the scene in the garden of Gethsemane, Luke declares " His sweat was as it were great drops of blood falling down to the ground." The writer to the Hebrews adds the significant detail that tears mingled with the blood. Already the Lord Jesus was feeling the weight of a world's iniquity; already He was beginning to taste the bitterness of His cup of sorrow. The garden conflict was the introductory stage of the triumph of the cross. The greatness of His desire to save the lost carried Him through that night of agony; but we shall never know how much our sins hurt the Son of God. It is significant that the Epistle to the Hebrews mentions " strong crying and tears." His anguish was not expressed in silent weeping, but in agonized sobs. " How greatly Jesus must have loved us."

PETER . . . who refused to have his feet washed
(JOHN 13:8)

All the major religions of the world are agreed on one basic fact. It is that man is a sinner and needs to be cleansed. All these faiths—Christianity excepted—are also agreed that man's cleansing depends upon his degree of merit. Man must *do* something in order to obtain forgiveness. The teachings of Christ are diametrically opposed to this, for He said that man's greatest efforts would be insufficient. Unless He cleansed men, they would not be clean.

The Sublime Saviour

The room was very still as every disciple watched the Lord. Tragedy seemed to hang in the air, and the idea of a kingdom was swiftly receding. The rugged disciples were beginning to realize that something was wrong. Anxiety clutched at their hearts as they saw the shadows gathering on the Master's face. He had risen from the table, and having girded Himself with a towel, He had placed a bowl of water on the floor, and was preparing to wash His followers' feet. Rather reluctantly the first disciple obeyed the Lord's invitation, and allowed Jesus to take hold of the travel-stained foot. The Lord tenderly washed away the dust, and then repeated the operation with the other foot. Radiantly He looked up into the face of His silent follower and then, carefully pushing the bowl along the floor, He prepared to wash the feet of the next disciple. The company was truly amazed, but only Simon Peter prepared to give utterance to his feelings.

The Stubborn Simon

" Then cometh He to Simon Peter: and Peter saith unto Him, Lord, dost thou wash my feet?" " Yes, Simon. You will not understand the meaning of this now, but soon all will be made perfectly clear to you." " Peter saith unto Him, Thou shalt never wash my feet." Slowly the Lord sat back on His heels and looked into the face of His determined friend. Peter's statement had electrified the atmosphere, for all the strained emotions of his soul had suddenly found an outlet. Perhaps there are two ways of interpreting

Peter's determination. Maybe he thought his feet were not needing to be washed; but more probably he considered himself unworthy of such attention. He was very determined, and had any other than the Lord been in charge of the situation, the position might have become grave. Calmly the Lord continued to watch His outspoken disciple, and then quietly He spoke again.

The Startling Statement

" Very well, Simon Peter; but ' If I wash thee not, thou hast no part with me.' Friend, all who belong to me *must be washed by me*. They cannot cleanse themselves. I must do it for them. I have already told you that what I do thou knowest not now; but thou shalt know hereafter. Therefore make your choice now. Submit and be washed, or go thy way—thou hast no part with me." And in those heart-searching moments, Peter's boisterous determination died within him. Had he been observant he might have seen the great satisfaction which suddenly shone in the Lord's eyes. It would appear that Christ succeeded in teaching far more truth through this one action than He had through all His sermons. In one delightful moment, He implanted seeds within their hearts which in after days would produce a great harvest of eternal blessing.

The Sensible Surrender

With great grace the Lord washed the feet of Peter and said, " He that is washed needeth not save to wash his feet." And His eyes seemed to add, " When a man has been really cleansed, his chief concern should be to attend to his daily walk." Peter was destined to remember that incident, and when at Pentecost the Holy Spirit came to lead him into the truth, he suddenly realized the imperativeness of being cleansed by the Saviour. Man at his best is still unclean, and needs to be washed by the Lord. As that realization burst upon his mind, Peter went out to preach, and his fiery utterances gained inspiration from the pre-Calvary scene. He cried, " Neither is there salvation in any other: for there is none other name under heaven given among men whereby we must be saved " (Acts 4:12).

THE DISCIPLE ... whom Jesus loved
(JOHN 13:23)

This statement indicates that John enjoyed a special place in the affections of the Saviour. The Master loved all His followers; yet for some undefined reason an inner circle of comradeship existed within the wider ranks of the disciples: only Peter, James, and John accompanied their Lord on certain missions. Yet it is most interesting to note that even within this inner circle of loyal friends, John occupied a place of pre-eminence. He became known as the disciple whom Jesus loved; and the statement suggests a challenging question. How did John gain this place of distinction in the affairs of his Master?

THE SPECIAL PLACE ... *He leaned upon the Master's bosom*
(JOHN 13:23)

" Now there was leaning on Jesus' bosom one of his disciples, whom Jesus loved." The Lord's intimation of the forthcoming betrayal shocked His followers, and they found it difficult to believe that one of their number would be a traitor. Spontaneously they cried, " Lord, is it I?" But it was left to John, who leaned against the Saviour's breast, to whisper the question, " Lord, who is it?" We read in the Gospel that the disciples quarrelled in regard to the seats of honour in the kingdom. Every man aspired to greatness, and the fact that two of their brotherhood had secretly conspired to obtain the places on either side of the throne, filled them with disgust. A first-class row seemed to be approaching, when Jesus gently intervened. Yet we do not read of their quarrelling in regard to the privilege of leaning on Christ's bosom. The disciples possibly considered John's action to be a little effeminate. He saw their frowns of displeasure, but remained indifferent to their scorn. He was not content to remain a yard away from his Lord when he could be near enough to hear the softest whisper.

THE SPECIAL PRIVILEGE ... " *Behold thy mother* "
(JOHN 19:26-27)

" When Jesus therefore saw his mother, and the disciple standing by, whom he loved, he saith unto his mother,

Woman, behold thy son! Then saith he to the disciple, Behold thy mother! And from that hour that disciple took her unto his own home." When Jesus entrusted his dearest earthly possession to the care of John, He conferred upon him the greatest honour. Yet with the honour went a great challenge, for John was asked to enter into the life of Mary to fill the vacancy caused by the death of Jesus. This was not an easy task; but when John's arm went around Mary's shoulders, it became obvious that he had accepted his Master's command. The Lord Jesus realized that John was completely trustworthy; His mother would be perfectly safe in the new home. Perhaps John's quiet contemplation on the bosom of Christ had prepared him for this great moment. Only those who have leaned on Christ's bosom are fit for the more intimate responsibilities of the kingdom.

THE SPECIAL PERCEPTION . . . "It is the Lord"
(JOHN 21:7)

The pale silvery light of a new dawn was slowly spreading over Galilee's waves when the tired fishermen brought their fishing vessel toward the beach. "Then Jesus saith unto them, Children, have ye any meat? They answered him, No. And He said unto them, Cast the net on the right side of the ship, and ye shall find. They cast therefore, and now they were not able to draw it for the multitude of fishes. Therefore that disciple whom Jesus loved saith unto Peter, It is the Lord." While the remaining disciples struggled with the fish, John calmly looked through the morning haze to recognize his Lord. He had very good eyesight! Neither the mists of the morning nor the storms of life could impair his vision. He occupied such a place of intimacy in the affections of the Lord Jesus that reciprocal love awarded him the great honour mentioned in the Scriptures. He became the disciple whom Jesus loved. There were three reasons why he deserved his reward. (i) When the other disciples thought of a kingdom, John drew nearer to Christ. (ii) When they ran for safety, John lingered at the cross to shelter a helpless woman. (iii) When they struggled to land a catch of fish, John forgot all earthly gains and rejoiced in the nearness of his Lord.

THE VINE . . . and the things which Christ cannot do !
(JOHN 15:1-5)

One of our popular hymns suggests, "There is nothing that Christ cannot do," and this thought is gladly accepted by the majority of Christians. We love to think that the affairs of daily life are in the hands of the omnipotent God; yet this confidence might be strangely related to fatalism. However comforting the thought may seem to be, the fact remains that there are certain things which He cannot accomplish in the experiences of His followers. These truths are clearly revealed in the parable of the vine.

The Vine Cannot Produce Fruit Without the Help of a Branch

The Lord Jesus said, "I am the vine, ye are the branches: He that abideth in me, and I in him, the same bringeth forth much fruit: for *without me ye can do nothing.*" We have only to change one letter and the final sentence would read, "without me He can do nothing." And that is true. Unless the vine can have the assistance of the branches, fruit-bearing will be an impossibility. The branch is the expression of the life of the tree, and by its co-operation the parent tree can fulfil its functions in life. The Saviour declared that what the branch is to the vine, so are we to Him. When He returned to heaven, He commissioned His disciples to go forth into all the world to preach the Gospel; and had they failed in their appointed task the cause of Christ would have been in jeopardy. The Lord Jesus needs men and women through whom to manifest Himself, and should these instruments prove to be unusable His purposes will be hindered. If there be but one Christian in an office, in a home, or in any other sphere, then quite obviously the Lord will be dependent upon the co-operation of that solitary follower.

The Vine Cannot Keep a Branch Healthy Unless it Imparts Life

The unhindered flow of life from the vine to the branch is absolutely essential if the health of the branch is to be maintained. If the life-channel should become blocked, or if for any other reason the sap ceases to flow, decay will immediately begin its work of destruction in the branch. Even so the Lord Jesus cannot maintain the life of His people unless He is able to fill them with His Spirit. The command of the Scripture is, " Be filled with the Spirit," and if any earthly hindrance interferes with that process, the health of the Christian is immediately endangered. A simple study of the ministry of the Lord will clearly reveal how He was filled with the Holy Spirit. He was born of the Spirit (Luke 1:35). After His baptism at the Jordan He was full of the Holy Spirit, and was led of the Spirit into the wilderness (Luke 4:1). He returned from His temptation in the power of the Spirit (Luke 4:14), and immediately claimed the fulfilment of Isaiah's prediction, for He said, " The Spirit of the Lord is upon me " (v. 18). He resisted all evil, and finally offered Himself through the eternal Spirit (Heb. 9:14). It is therefore clear that the divine Spirit completely filled the vine; and unless Christ can likewise fill us, decay will quickly become apparent.

The Vine Cannot Prevent the Useless Branch Becoming a Castaway

" If a man abide not in me, he is cast forth as a branch, and is withered; and men gather them, and cast them into the fire, and they are burned " (John 15:6). If a branch is proved to be useless, nothing can prevent its removal from the sphere of service. We do well to consider that a man's eternal destiny is not the theme of this discourse, for Christ had already declared that no one could pluck the saint from the hand of His Father. The theme in this parable is fruit-fulness in the vineyard of God. Every Christian should bear fruit for the Master; but if sin and self should ruin my fruit-bearing potentialities, God will remove me lest I become a hindrance to others. Disease can easily spread among fruit trees, and with so much at stake, the great Husbandman will resolutely remove all hindrances. The ingathering of the eternal harvest must not be endangered. Even Paul recognized the possibility of becoming a cast-away (1 Cor. 9:27). Haunting memories of a lost opportunity are the only clouds that might hide temporarily the glory of the eternal sunshine.

JOHN . . . and the way to supreme happiness

The apostle John had an infallible remedy for happiness. It was a guaranteed cure for melancholia, and promised complete satisfaction to any man or woman who would give it a fair trial. Yet he was unable to claim proprietary rights for his prescription, as he had learned his secrets from Another. He had lived with the Great Physician, and his opportunities for study had not been neglected.

Ingredient 1. I Must Abide in Christ

" Abide in me, and I in you. As the branch cannot bear fruit of itself, except it abide in the vine; no more can ye, except ye abide in me. . . . These things have I spoken unto you, that my joy might remain in you, and *that your joy might be full*" (John 15:4, 11). Supreme happiness only becomes possible for the Christian when he learns to abide in his Lord. Should anything prevent the flow of life from the Lord to His child—from the vine to the branch—spiritual tragedy will undoubtedly follow. The health of the branch is dependent upon clean channels through which the life-giving sap might flow. And in like manner this is true of the relationship between Christ and His followers.

Ingredient 2. I Must Commune With Christ

" Verily, verily, I say unto you, Whatsoever ye shall ask the Father in my name, He will give it you. Hitherto have ye asked nothing in my name: ask, and ye shall receive, *that your joy may be full*" (John 16:23, 24). This constituted the new teaching on prayer. Through the medium of Christ the disciples could talk with God, and confidently expect to receive from Him definite answers to their petitions. When humble fishermen found in the Lord Jesus the authority and means whereby to approach the throne of grace, they quickly discovered that language was inadequate to express the joy resulting from a real answer to prayer.

Ingredient 3. I Must Study the Words of Christ

" And now come I to thee; and these things I speak in the world, *that they might have my joy fulfilled in them-*

selves. I have given them thy word . . ." (John 17:13, 14). The immortal prayer of Christ reveals many truths, but this is one of the greatest. We may never know how often Jesus secretly prayed in the mountains, for He constantly sought the place of communion. Yet in the garden of Gethsemane the Lord ordained that His prayer should be made public, in order that the disciples might have access to His words. He desired that they should be acquainted with His statements, for through this medium abundant joy would reach their hearts. His gracious words are now recorded in a book which is a source of real happiness to every devout reader.

Ingredient 4. *I Must Walk With Christ*

"That which we have seen and heard declare we unto you, that ye also may have fellowship with us: and truly our fellowship is with the Father, and with his Son Jesus Christ. And these things write we unto you, *that your joy may be full.* . . . Walk in the light" (I John 1:3-7). It remains one of the greatest miracles of our faith that through His death and resurrection, the Saviour has now become omnipresent to His people. He has said, "I will never leave you." And if this be true, we are thereby provided with the opportunity of walking with Him in blessed fellowship. The road of life need never be lonely. Every path can be an Emmaus road, on which our hearts may burn as we listen to His word.

Ingredient 5. *I Must Talk About Christ*

"Having many things to write unto you, I would not write with paper and ink: but I trust to come unto you, and speak face to face, *that our joy may be full*" (2 John 12). This is a fitting climax for all that has gone before. If we enjoy the preliminary steps, we cannot refrain from talking about the Lord Jesus. It is easy for us to imagine John sitting down with the "elect lady and her children," and as they conversed about the Saviour, their faces shone with holy delight.

THE CROWNS OF THE SAVIOUR . . . and
how He received them
(JOHN 19:2)

This is a most interesting study, for there are three places in Holy Scripture where the Lord Jesus is said to be crowned. When viewed together, these texts provide a comprehensive picture of the purposes of God in man's salvation. We find in John 19:2 that Jesus of Nazareth was crowned with thorns; and that revelation sums up the account of the Christ of yesterday. He is the source of all true happiness. Hebrews 2:9 reveals that Christ is now crowned in heaven, where at the right hand of His Father He intercedes on behalf of all His people. That truly expresses the Christ of today, and suggests the source of unfailing help. The last picture is described in Revelation 19:12, where the apostle John declares: " And on his head were many crowns." This expresses all the teaching concerning the Christ of the future. The statement, " We see Jesus . . . crowned " can be an enthralling text.

Jesus . . . Crowned With Thorns

" And the soldiers platted a crown of thorns, and put it on His head, and they put on Him a purple robe, and said, Hail, King of the Jews." The irresponsible actions of these men were almost prophetic. Actuated by thoughts of brutal persecution, they thought only of the fierce pleasure which their victim would provide. In order to express the hidden meanings of divine revelation, no action would have been better suited to the moment. Thorns were never meant to be a part of God's world, and only appeared when sin had marred God's handiwork. They were the emblems of sin. In their blind and wilful ignorance the soldiers crowned Jesus with the evidences of a world's guilt. Their actions were indeed prophetic, and within a short space of time, God fulfilled their prediction. He took—not the emblem of sin, but the sin itself, and made it to rest upon the head of His beloved Son. " The Lord hath laid on him the iniquity of us all." Therein lies the secret of man's happiness

Jesus . . . Crowned With Glory and Honour

" But now we see not yet all things put under him. But

135

we see Jesus, who was made a little lower than the angels . . . crowned with glory and honour." The Christ of yesterday may appear to be a wonderful Saviour, but if the Gospel contains nothing more, it can be of little use to present-day men and women. The writer to the Hebrews continues the story and describes how the Lord Jesus ascended to the right hand of the majesty on high, to be crowned with glory. The eternal Father said, " Sit on my right hand, until I make thine enemies thy footstool," and while all the assembled hosts of heaven watched, He crowned the Lord Jesus with glory and honour. The epistle to the Hebrews teaches that Christ ever liveth to make intercession for us, and we may draw near in full assurance of faith and find grace to help us in time of need. If the reconciliation accomplished at the cross brings happiness, the intercession at God's right hand brings help to all who believe.

Jesus . . . Crowned With Many Crowns

"And I saw heaven opened, and behold a white horse; and he that sat upon him was called Faithful and True. . . . His eyes were as a flame of fire, and on his head were many crowns. . . . And he was clothed with a vesture dipped in blood: and his name is called The Word of God. . . . And he had on his vesture and on his thigh a name written, KING OF KINGS AND LORD OF LORDS." From his island prison, the apostle John saw " the things to be hereafter," and his soul-thrilling vision revealed that in the closing moments of time the Lord Jesus would return to earth to reign among His people. The kingdoms of the world would be His domain, and " the tabernacle of God shall be among men." The hymnist has conjectured that the accumulation of crowns expresses the fact that the saints will have already presented their rewards to their Saviour. John undoubtedly thought of the kingdoms become the possession of Christ. Yet the supreme fact seems to be that the eternal home of all who love the Saviour will be found in those days. The Christ of the future transcends all else, and every true Christian exclaims " Even so, come, Lord Jesus."

MARY MAGDALENE . . . who was told to keep her distance

(John 20:17)

The Lord Jesus Christ did and said many strange things, and every day promised new and exciting experiences to the men who followed Him. Yet even they must have been greatly surprised when they heard of His command to the beloved Magdalene. It was Easter Sunday morning when the faithful woman went down to the tomb. Dismayed at the thought that someone had stolen the Lord's body, she asked one whom she supposed to be the gardener, if he had taken away the body; and while she awaited an answer, she suddenly heard the Master's voice, and recognized her Lord. Instinctively she fell at His feet to worship Him; but as she reached out her hands, He said, " Touch me not; for I am not yet ascended to my Father." It seems that later she was permitted to touch Him, but the initial command brought an entirely new note into the teaching of Jesus.

The New Command

The key message of Christ's ministry had been, " Come unto me . . . and I will give you rest." When a leper fell at His feet, the Saviour stretched forth a hand and *touched* Him. Just one week after meeting Magdalene, He invited Thomas to place a finger into the mark of the nail; and to say the least, His denial to Magdalene seems as strange as His invitation to Thomas seems unfair. Why did Christ tell the woman to keep her distance? The text obviously supplies the answer. " I am not yet ascended to my Father." There is a threefold newness of relationship here, and we do well to notice it. (i) *A new relationship between man and Christ*. Something had happened to Jesus, for whereas He had formerly invited people to draw near, now He forbade His disciple to touch Him. Calvary had altered the Saviour's attitude. (ii) *A new relationship between Christ and God*. On that Easter day, neither communion in the mount nor the promise of an imminent departure for heaven would suffice. It had become immediately necessary to present Himself before the Almighty. Why? (iii) *A new relationship between God and man*. The Fatherhood of God takes the pre-eminent place in the Gospel. " I ascend unto MY FATHER and YOUR FATHER, and to my God and your God." Therefore it is clear that the first thing Jesus did on that memorable day was to ascend into the immediate presence of God.

The New Credentials

When an ambassador has been appointed to a foreign court, his first duty is that of presenting his credentials to the reigning sovereign. Until these have been accepted, he has no authority to represent his people in that land. The same thought is expressed in the Old Testament teaching concerning the high priesthood of Israel. Before the priest could represent the people, he himself had to be accepted by God. Then the blood of the offering would be sprinkled on the mercy seat, and the appointed man could act on behalf of his nation. The epistle to the Hebrews clearly reveals that Christ is now our accepted High Priest. His death at Calvary fulfilled every type concerning the blood of the lamb, and the only thing that remained to be accomplished was the presentation of His credentials before the throne of God. Therefore on that Easter day the scene in heaven beggared description, for all the angelic host watched the eternal Son presenting before His Father the evidence of His sufferings.

The New Challenge

" Then the same day at evening . . . came Jesus and stood in the midst, and saith unto them, Peace be unto you. And when He had so said, He shewed unto them His hands and His side. Then were the disciples glad when they saw the Lord." It was as though He said, " Can you see these wounds in my hands and my side? They were the credentials which I presented on your behalf in heaven. My Father accepted them; will you?" Thomas was not present at that meeting, but all his doubts were banished eight days later, when the Saviour invited him saying, " Thomas, reach hither thy finger, and behold my hands; and reach hither thy hand, and thrust it into my side: and be not faithless, but believing." This constituted the new challenge. Here we have blessing in triplicate. The disciples looked at the Lord and discovered a new *peace*. " Peace be unto you." They recognized the way of *pardon*. " He shewed unto them His hands." They experienced *pleasure*. " Then were the disciples glad, when they saw the Lord."

THE BEGGAR . . . who asked for alms and was given legs

"And a certain man lame from his mother's womb was carried, whom they laid daily at the gate of the temple which is called Beautiful, to ask alms of them that entered into the temple." A poor frustrated man, he lay on his couch at the side of the street, and all who visited the temple saw him as he stretched out his hand for gifts. He was alive, but he was not healthy. His heart beat fast, but his feet never moved. He had been lame from his birth. There were days when he heard the chanting of the psalms in the nearby temple, and watched the priests as they walked to and fro. He was very near to the place of blessing, but he never reached it. He knew all the details of the service schedule, and could have given precise information concerning the ritual of the house of God. He had many friends who frequented the sanctuary, yet he remained on his couch in the street. He begged before and after services, and constantly hoped that devotion would loosen the strings of purses. Poor man: he lay within reach of a gold mine, yet he only gathered pennies!

Sitting by the Street

He seems singularly interesting to us, for we are confronted by a great question: "Can a Christian be lame from his birth?" Is it possible to be spiritually alive and not to be healthy? Is it possible to have a warm heart, and at the same time to possess paralysed feet? Both the Bible and human experience answer "yes." A man may believe in the Lord Jesus Christ, and subscribe to all the doctrines of grace, yet not be useful in the kingdom of God. The apostle Paul continually urged his converts to walk worthily of their high calling, but it was impossible to do this on feet that would not respond. The ancient beggar seems very modern. There are many people who know a great deal about life in the holy place; they can even describe its details; but theirs is only an intellectual apprehension, for in actual experience they listen from a distance. Their real interest lies in the street, where materialistic delights exercise a strangle-hold upon every spiritual inclination.

Probably the beggar had more money than Peter, for the apostle confessed, " Silver and gold have I none." Yet the follower of Christ possessed something unobtainable in the markets of the world. These two men are best appreciated together. The outstretched hand of the beggar contrasts with the overflowing soul of the great preacher. " Then Peter said, Silver and gold have I none; but such as I have give I thee: In the name of Jesus Christ of Nazareth rise up and walk. And he took him by the right hand and lifted him· up: and immediately his feet and ankle bones received strength." In the following moments the old desires fell away as though they had been a mantle, and rising above the limitations of his couch, he walked in newness of life. He had been alive for years, but suddenly with refreshing power, abundant life came to flood his being. The story perfectly illustrates the transformation which takes place when the Holy Spirit comes to heal and restore and control the child of God.

Singing in the Sanctuary

" And he leaping up stood, and walked, and entered with them into the temple, walking, and leaping, and praising God." As the crowd hurried to see the man who had been so wonderfully healed, and as the man himself stayed close by his new friends, Peter said, " Why look ye so earnestly upon us, as though by our own power or holiness we had made this man to walk? The God of Abraham . . . hath glorified his Son Jesus . . . and hath made this man strong." And from that day the beggar's couch disappeared from the gateway of the temple. Radiant activity removed for ever the necessity to lie in the dust begging. The songs of the sanctuary re-echoed the music of his heart, as the power of a risen Saviour became a reality in his experience. We see again the carnal Christian who sits in his lameness seeking the things of earth; we see also the Spirit-filled saint. There is all the difference in the world between these two men; but it is not difficult to decide which is the more pleasing to his Lord. The man who sits with his back to the altar will always have trouble with his feet. It is grand to be alive, but it is better to be healthy.

THE PRIESTS . . . who took a long time to decide for Christ (Acts 6:7)

" And the word of God increased; and the number of the disciples multiplied in Jerusalem greatly; *and a great company of the priests were obedient to the faith.*" It is not unlikely that the final statement in this verse represents a triumph of patient perseverance in the art of soul-winning.

Testimony 1. Matthew 8:4

Perhaps some of the priests were sitting around their table when the ominous knock sounded at the door. Someone was in a hurry! When one of the number opened the door, he saw a rather dilapidated beggar—or so he thought. He cynically smiled. Here was another fellow who thought the priests were millionaires! " Yes, and what do you want? " " I want to give you something, sir. Moses said that if a leper were cleansed he should offer certain things according to the law, and I want to do that." The words tumbled from the man's lips, and he seemed possessed by a strange excitement. The priest looked at him. A leper— cleansed—what nonsense! " Yes, priest, I was a leper without hope when Jesus found me. Perhaps I should say that I found Him, for I ran and fell at His feet and said, ' Lord, if thou wilt, thou canst make me clean,' and He touched me, and I was cleansed immediately. Then He reminded me of my duty to go to the priests; and here I am." When the priest had attended to the requirements of the stranger, he returned to his colleagues; and that evening they surely had great discussions. Then, as always, it was one thing to dismiss Jesus of Nazareth as a fanatical imposter, but quite another to account for the wonder of His miracles.

Testimony 2. Luke 17:14

The priest could hardly believe his ears. Nine men standing around the doorway maintained they had all been lepers. They were very poor; their garments were tattered, and everything about their appearance suggested hardship —but lepers, No! " Yes, sir, we were all lepers; and we stood and cried, ' Jesus, Master, have mercy on us.' He heard us, and told us to come and see you." " And were you healed then? " " No, sir, we heard His voice but we were still lepers. Yet He commanded us to come. We obeyed, and as we walked along the street, a new healing power came into our bodies and we were made clean." Some time later the priest was recalled to the door, to find another man who claimed he was the tenth of the original party. He had returned to Christ to give Him thanks, and was a little late in presenting himself before the priest. He reiterated all that had already been told to the leader, and once again the great men of the temple faced the challenge of the Nazarene. We shall never know how near they came to believing in Christ at that time; but when Jesus died, it seemed that the new movement would die with Him.

Testimony 3. *Acts* 3 : 1-8

It was the hour of prayer, and some of the priests would be officiating within the sacred house. Outside, the city was agog with excitement. People were saying that Jesus of Nazareth had risen from the dead, and great public meetings had brought the enthusiasm of the crowds to fever pitch. Everywhere men and women talked of the great occurrence, and it was being rumoured that thousands of converts had been won for the new movement. The priests waited expectantly, for some of the strange preachers would be coming to pray. Suddenly there was a great commotion outside the building, and as the door opened, the waiting men saw a great crowd being led by an apparently hysterical man who jumped, and danced, and shouted. " And they knew that it was he which sat for alms at the Beautiful gate of the temple: and they were filled with wonder and amazement at that which had happened unto him." When Peter explained how the lame man had been made whole, the priests realized that once again the power of Jesus had been made manifest. And this time the great leaders refused to postpone their decision. They could not remain secret followers of Christ when their hearts thrilled at the mention of His name. That day they left all, and followed the Saviour. And the moral of the story for all soul-winners is, " If at first you don't succeed, try, try again."

CORNELIUS . . . the soldier who was baptized twice

Dear Cornelius,

You are among the select band of ancient saints with whom so many of us would like to speak. The story of your sending to Simon Peter has been carefully preserved in the Scriptures, and today millions of people are acquainted with the details of your remarkable conversion. We like you! Yes, there can never be any question about that fact, for you have completely won our admiration. We are particularly thrilled to know that in God's estimation you were " a devout man, and one that feared God with all his house, which gave much alms to the people, and prayed to God alway " (Acts 10:2). That is a noble record, and places you among the aristocracy of the ancient world.

The Gentile Believer

We have noted with great interest that you were a centurion of the Italian band. That means, of course, that you were a Gentile soldier who had been posted to the Palestinian garrison. Naturally, we would expect to discover that in common with your race, you would worship idols. It was rather startling to find you were already a believer in the true God. And that is where our questioning would begin. When and where did you renounce your former faith?—for we assume that you were once an idolater. Were there Jews in Italy, and had their teaching influenced you in the supreme matters of religion and life? What happened among your friends when you renounced idols? Did your decision lead to unpleasant repercussions in your military career? Obviously the beauty of the law of Moses gripped your heart, and perhaps even your critics were influenced by your high standard of morality. We have not forgotten that it is also said, " Thy prayers and thine alms are come up for a memorial before God " (v. 4).

The Greater Blessedness

Sir, perhaps we are mistaken in our conjecture, but it seems to us that in spite of your great achievements and unquestioned virtue, you were equally conscious of a growing need in your soul. Were you not seeking from God an indefinable something which would lead to inward satisfaction? Anyhow, that is how it appears to us, for when God answered your prayer, you were instructed to send for a Gospel preacher. You remind us of the rich young ruler who once conversed with the Saviour. He also had kept the law, but had suddenly realized he still needed to inherit eternal life. Yes, we have carefully noted how God sent His messages both to you and the leader of the Church; we have observed how Peter's vision was timed perfectly to coincide with the arrival of your messengers. Cornelius, doesn't God plan things well! And then Simon arrived at your home to discover an audience waiting to hear whatsoever would be said. We are not told that you made any decision for Christ, for while the sermon was still being preached, " the Holy Spirit fell on all them which heard the word." Could you explain that to us, Cornelius? Had you secretly believed in Christ before that moment, or did the revelation suddenly come to your soul?

The Glorious Baptism

Do you still remember how your illustrious preacher said, " Can any man forbid water, that these should not be baptized, which have received the Holy Spirit as well as we?" What were your feelings, dear brother, when Simon Peter commanded you to be baptized? Probably this was the second occasion for you to be immersed. The Jewish leaders baptized you when you renounced idols. It was your confession that you had finished with idolatry, and that you intended to live a new life. So you really understood what Peter meant when he gave his command. Where did that Christian baptism take place, Cornelius? Did you go to the seaside, or to the river, and did many people gather around to witness your public confession of the Lord Jesus Christ? Ah well, sometime we may have a chance to speak together of these wonderful experiences, and then you will undoubtedly tell us many things we wish to know. And in return, dear brother, we will tell you how God found us. Cornelius, in that glad day we shall forget all about visions, for our faith will give place to sight. We shall see the King in His beauty.

MANAEN . . . the prince who became a preacher

" Now there were in the church that was at Antioch certain prophets and teachers; as Barnabas, and Simeon that was called Niger, and Lucius of Cyrene, *and Manaen, the foster brother of Herod the tetrarch,* and Saul." All these were great leaders of the Church, but not the least among them was the little-known Manaen, about whom an interesting story has been told. Josephus, the Jewish historian, relates that when the first Herod was a child, a prophet named Manahem foretold his accession to the throne. " Now at that time, Herod did not at all attend to what Manahem had said, as having no hopes of such advancement; but a little after, when he was so fortunate as to be advanced to the dignity of king, and was in the height of his dominion, he sent for Manahem, and asked him how long he should reign " (Antiquities of the Jews. Book 15, chapter 8, paragraph 5). It has been suggested that as a mark of royal gratitude, the king adopted the prophet's son Manaen, and that this was the boy who long afterward became a deacon in the Church at Antioch.

The Discontented Prince

If the details of the ancient story be correct, it would be interesting to know what length of time elapsed before the glamour of court life ceased to charm this son of the manse. Probably the ceaseless whirl of gaiety fascinated him, and provided a striking contrast to the limited entertainments of his old home. Laughter, new friends, and a plentiful supply of money, were great assets; yet there came a day when Manaen became conscious of a deeper hunger, of an intense yearning to find something which would satisfy the inherent longings of his heart. Herod's murder of John Baptist revived memories of his own father, and Manaen realized that had it been possible, Manahem would have joined in the fearless denunciation of the king's conduct. And as the glamour of frivolity began to disappear, the dissatisfaction of this young man constantly increased. He was beginning to discover that abiding peace was a rare gem; that a man must visit the wells of God's salvation before he can find springs of eternal refreshment capable of meeting every need.

The Discerning Penitent

And then came Jesus of Nazareth! Every day the crowds flocked to hear the new Teacher; and every day, new stories of triumphant grace circulated throughout the nation. Did Manaen join the eager throng to hear the Saviour? Already the impact of the Lord's message had been felt in court circles, for Joanna, the wife of the prime minister, had responded to the call of Christ. It would not be possible for this unhappy prince to hear the word of God and not to feel a resurgence of the old emotions. Jesus of Nazareth spoke of God, of eternity, of life; and every sincere heart answered His call. How we would love to question Manaen! Did he come, as the nobleman, to the feet of Jesus? Did he pour out his soul in earnest supplication? And when he eventually renounced the sinful associations of palace life, did the news of his conversion thrill or shock the nation?

The Distinguished Preacher

And so Herod's foster-brother became a Christian; and it is most inspiring to discover that amid the leaders of the Church at Antioch, the one-time prince had an honoured place. Indeed, he had a part in sending out the first Christian missionaries, for as the prophets and teachers of Antioch " ministered to the Lord, and fasted, the Holy Spirit said, Separate me Barnabas and Saul for the work whereunto I have called them." Manaen left his society friends, and found new companions among the humble followers of the Saviour. The pomp and splendid magnificence of the old life became a memory as he dressed in the unpretentious garments of an ordinary man. The ostentatious superficiality of princelings faded into insignificance as he walked with God. The new message became the delight of his heart, and his educational attainments were used to advantage when he began to instruct his new friends in the ways and wisdom of God. Soon the Christian prince was known to all the brethren, and ultimately he was advanced to a place of eminence in the councils of the Church.

What a wonderful change in my life has been wrought
Since Jesus came into my heart.

SOSTHENES . . . one of Paul's most remarkable converts

The authorities of the synagogue were worried, and their fears were not groundless. Paul, who had been in their city for some time, had been joined by two of his colleagues. An added impetus had been given to the zeal of the fearless preacher, and the leaders of Israel dreaded the possibilities of the immediate future. "And when they opposed themselves, and blasphemed, Paul shook his raiment, and said unto them, Your blood be upon your own heads; I am clean: from henceforth I will go unto the Gentiles " (Acts 18:6). They watched as he entered into the nearby house of Justus, but their anger deepened when they discovered that a great change had taken place in their own leader. "And Crispus, *the chief ruler of the synagogue,* believed on the Lord with all his house" (v. 8).

The Unique Task

During the following days, the cause of Israel seemed in jeopardy, and the people were at wits' end to know what to do. Someone had to be found who would challenge and overcome the threat of the Christian faith. Some strong character had to counteract the influence of the terrible visitor! When Sosthenes succeeded to the rulership of the synagogue, it appeared that such a man had been found. He would stand no nonsense! He was a man who would fiercely use any means, legitimate or otherwise, in order to attain his purpose. It was not a cause for amazement, therefore, when the new leader organized a great demonstration before the authorities. "And when Gallio was the deputy of Achaia, the Jews made insurrection with one accord against Paul, and brought him to the judgment seat " (v. 12). Their riotous behaviour stirred the entire city, and many Greeks also attended the trial. At first it seemed most probable that Paul would be sentenced for disturbing the peace; but to the astonishment of Israel, the judge ignored their protests and dismissed the case. When they would have argued, the soldiers forcibly removed them from the court, and "all the Greeks took Sosthenes, the chief ruler of the synagogue, and beat him before the judgment seat. And Gallio cared for none of those things."

The Unmerciful Thrashing

So ended one of the most momentous days in the stormy experiences of Paul. Probably he also watched, as the enemy of his faith was beaten by the crowd. Many of the Christians might have felt elated at the amazing turn of events; but Paul was sad. Ultimately the mob allowed the assaulted ruler to escape to his home, and while they went laughing on their way, the poor Jew prostrated himself upon his bed. His schemings had failed entirely; his pride had suffered irreparable damage, and even the cause of Israel had been brought into disfavour. Was it at that moment that Paul knocked at the door? Of course we cannot be sure of these things, but since this eminent Jew became a great Christian (1 Cor. 1:1) we are at least justified in asking if he were won for Christ through the ministry of his one-time enemy? Did the apostle quietly enter, to attend to the wounds of the man who had sought his destruction? Did the graciousness and sincerity of the man of Tarsus overcome all the prejudice and animosity of Sosthenes?

The Unexpected Testimony

Years later, when Paul wrote to the Church in Corinth, he was able to say, " Paul, called to be an apostle of Jesus Christ through the will of God, and *Sosthenes our brother.* Unto the church of God which is at Corinth . . . Grace be unto you." Obviously there is a gap between the two sections of the story; but it is clear that the old enemy of the faith, the one-time ruler of the synagogue, had taken his place at Paul's side. In company with his predecessor Crispus, Sosthenes had bowed before the Lord Jesus Christ, and through personal faith in the Saviour had found peace beyond understanding. It would appear that two features united to win him for Christ. Paul's loving deeds had adorned the Gospel he proclaimed, and this combination of virtues swept aside all opposition, and brought Sosthenes to the Lord. The story is rich in suggestions, but perhaps the greatest is that we should never despair of winning difficult characters, for oftentimes the most unlikely people become the best Christians.

APOLLOS . . . in whose fiery sermons something was lacking (Acts 18:25)

" And a certain Jew named Apollos, born at Alexandria, an eloquent man, and mighty in the Scriptures, came to Ephesus. This man was instructed in the way of the Lord; and being fervent in the spirit, he spake and taught diligently the things of the Lord, knowing only the baptism of John." The coming of this remarkable man seemed a God-send to the harassed, persecuted Christians. He was a most able scholar, whose fiery eloquence electrified meetings and confounded the most bitter critics. He seemed to be the answer to the Christians' prayers. Yet while all this excitement prevailed in the hearts of the Ephesian Christians, two thoughtful people recognized that something was wrong with the young preacher. His message was expressed in words of fire; his knowledge of the prophets was far above the ordinary; yet, somewhere, something was lacking.

The Great Scholar

" He was mighty in the Scriptures." Such great knowledge could not have been acquired in a moment. His parents were probably devout Jews, whose boy had been taught in the Scriptures " from his youth up." When Apollos passed from youth to manhood, the influence of the law and the prophets dominated his entire thought. The coming of Jesus of Nazareth had been the fulfilment of the ancient predictions; the Jewish rejection of their Messiah had been the greatest national mistake, and unless Israel repented of sin, the outpouring of God's wrath would be inevitable. The cry of John Baptist needed to be repeated in every village of the land. Whenever Apollos read his Scripture, every prophetic utterance emphasized the importance of this fact, and finally the young man could say, with Jeremiah, " But his word was in mine heart as a burning fire shut up in my bones . . . and I could not stay " (Jer. 20:9).

The Great Speaker

" He was an eloquent man . . . instructed in the way of the Lord; and being fervent in the spirit, he spake and taught diligently . . ." The thrilling, passionate preaching of this young man seemed a refreshing breeze on a sultry, stifling afternoon. It revived drooping spirits, and gave promise of a new leader whose exploits would lead to greater conquests in the name of the Lord. The Christians were thrilled at the prospect of every new oration, and their hearts readily responded to the way in which he marshalled his prophetic facts. He was a genius, and "mightily convinced the Jews, and that publickly, shewing by the Scriptures that Jesus was Christ." Yet all the while, the cross of Calvary represented nothing but the overwhelming folly of Israel. They had crucified their Messiah, and had lost their greatest opportunity. That God was in Christ reconciling the world to Himself, was a truth unknown to Apollos. His passionate outpourings were expressive of his deep sincerity, but his Messiah was dead; for even if Jesus of Nazareth had risen again, He had now returned to heaven, and Israel's opportunity had gone with Him. Repentance alone could prevent the doom of the nation.

The Great Saint

"Aquila and Priscilla . . . took him unto them, and expounded unto him the way of God more perfectly." It is a cause for pleasure that the Scriptures declare that both man and wife helped to instruct this brilliant young man. Undoubtedly the husband led the discussion, but whenever he failed to make a point in a way satisfactory to his wife, she joined in the conversation, and her contributions added charm and value to the evening. Ultimately a new revelation changed the entire outlook of the young preacher, "And when he was disposed to pass into Achaia, the brethren wrote, exhorting the disciples to receive him . . ." Eventually Apollos reached Corinth, where Paul had founded a Church on the doctrines of redemption. He had determined to know nothing among the people save "Christ and Him crucified." That the Church responded to the preaching of the young visitor proves how well Aquila and Priscilla had done their work. A live coal from off the altar had touched his heart and his lips; he also preached reconciliation through the cross, and was a worthy man to follow in the footsteps of their beloved Paul.

AGRIPPA . . . who lost the chance of a lifetime

(Acts 26:28)

The scene was set for one of the greatest trials in history. Preliminary investigations had been completed, and with the arrival of King Agrippa the time seemed opportune to settle Paul's case once and for ever. "And on the morrow, when Agrippa was come, and Bernice, with great pomp, and was entered into the place of hearing, with the chief captains, and principal men of the city, at Festus' commandment Paul was brought forth. And Festus said, King Agrippa, and all men which are here present with us, ye see this man, about whom all the multitude of the Jews have dealt with me, both at Jerusalem, and also here, crying that he ought not to live any longer" (Acts 25:23, 24). Intense silence greeted the statement, and every eye was turned toward Paul when Agrippa ultimately said, "Paul, thou art permitted to speak for thyself" (26:1).

The King Who Recognized the Truth

Paul's shrewd eyes recognized that his illustrious judge was no stranger to the ways and beliefs of Israel. He said, "I think myself happy, king Agrippa, because . . . I know thee to be *expert in all customs and questions which are among the Jews*: wherefore I beseech thee to hear me patiently" (v. 3). Later, when the speaker had told his remarkable story, his impassioned voice cried, "King Agrippa, believest thou the prophets? *I know that thou believest*" (v. 27). These two statements reveal that the judge was acquainted with the holy Scriptures. His constant interest in the life of the nation had made him expert in all Hebrew affairs. It would also follow that he knew about the Lord Jesus, and the ways of the Christian Church, for when Festus accused Paul of madness, the prisoner replied, "I am not mad, most noble Festus; but speak forth the words of truth and soberness. For the king knoweth of these things, before whom also I speak freely: for I am persuaded that *none of these things are hidden from him;* for this thing was not done in a corner."

The King Who Resisted the Truth

Perhaps we shall never be sure why Agrippa replied, "Almost thou persuadest me to be a Christian." It has been suggested this was an answer of mockery, and meant "With such little persuasion, would you try to convert me?" Yet, a man expert in Jewish ways; a man who believed in the hope of Israel; and one who had heard the testimony of the great Paul, could hardly scorn such a wonderful message. Each reader must decide for himself what Agrippa really meant; but one thing is above dispute. At least the king realized what it meant to be a Christian, and confessed he had not yet become one. Whether he was near or far from the place of surrender, he had seen a vision of the power of God, and the extent of Christ's Kingdom. Christians were people who owned no other Master. No man can follow Christ without becoming conscious of a duty to bear a cross daily. If Agrippa supported this cause, unpleasant repercussions would be known throughout the nation. A royal conversion would be a sensation, and would necessitate many fundamental changes in the king's conduct.

The King Who Renounced the Truth

Beyond the bounds of that court-house, heaven waited for the royal verdict. The court adjourned, and Agrippa, Bernice, and Festus, went aside to discuss their findings. They agreed that the prisoner was innocent, but excused their inaction by saying, "This man might have been set at liberty, if he had not appealed unto Caesar" (v. 32). And possibly had Caesar been present he would have dismissed them for their willingness to waste money in transporting a prisoner and his escort to Rome, when according to their own statements he was guiltless. This story has bequeathed to posterity three vital suggestions. (i) *The inevitability of decision.* Every man challenged by the Gospel of Christ makes a decision, whether he wants to or not. (ii) *The inadvisability of delay.* To plan a future decision is to provide evidence of folly. The future is unknown. (iii) *The inexorability of death.* The last enemy of sinful man is always triumphant. All men must die, "and after death the judgment." When Agrippa turned away from the Christian preacher, he turned away from Christ.

Poor Agrippa, he was so near to the Kingdom of God, but he missed the chance of a lifetime!

THE SHIP'S CREW . . . which nearly committed suicide
(Acts 27:12)

The sailing ship seemed to be hugging the coast, for her captain was a very worried man. Unusual delays had placed the ship behind schedule, and with the approach of the stormy season, the time for sailing had gone. Constantly, anxious eyes scanned the horizon, and many silent prayers were offered for the safety of the vessel. When the famous headlands came into view, the captain sighed with hope and eagerness. If only he could reach the desired refuge in time! Freshening winds filling the canvas gladdened his heart, and slowly the vessel sailed onward. "And when we had sailed slowly many days . . . we came unto a place which is called The fair havens; nigh whereunto was the city of Lasea " (Acts 27:7-8).

Sure Delights

" The fair havens " was a pretty name; it would be interesting to know who first so named the picturesque harbour. Probably many storm-tossed mariners had sought sanctuary on its placid waters, and one of them had expressed his appreciation when He said, " This is a fair haven." Others shared his opinion, and with the passing of time the place became known as " The fair havens." We could ask what has been its counterpart in the history of mankind? The greatest storms of life are not always confined to oceans and continents. Some are found within the hearts of men and women. We might profitably enquire the location of the harbour into which our forefathers ran their storm-tossed vessels. And the answer would be instantly forthcoming. The Church of God has always been the place where travellers found rest. There, innumerable fleets of human vessels found a safe anchorage; and there, hearts have been at rest.

Strange Desires

" And because the haven was not commodious to winter in, the more part advised to depart thence also, if by any means they might attain to Phenice, and there to winter . . ." (v. 12). A man's vision is often affected by the desires of his heart. One looked at the fair havens and saw the tranquillity and peace of a lovely harbour. Another looked and saw a lonely place five miles from the nearest centre of habitation. Mutinous thoughts filled the hearts of the crew as they longed for the taverns and gaiety of Phenice . . . the city of palm trees. A deputation waited upon the captain, and their ideas were forcefully presented. The anchor was lifted, and in spite of Paul's warning the ship put to sea. In like manner, many people have left the fair havens of God's house because they have considered it to be too small to accommodate all their desires. Soft lights and sweet music must be sought over the sea in Phenice. The fair havens may be all right, but . . .

Startling Distress

" And when the south wind blew softly, supposing that they had obtained their purpose, loosing thence, they sailed close by Crete. But not long after there arose against it a tempestuous wind called Euroclydon . . . And when neither sun nor stars in many days appeared, and no small tempest lay on us, all hope that we should be saved was then taken away " (vv. 13-20). And amid the despair of the storm, the peace of the fair havens appeared as one of the most-to-be-desired treasures in the world. How stupid they had been ever to leave the shelter of that delightful place! Our world is filled with people who have similarly made a great mistake. They have left the security of the harbour of God, and in search of worldly pleasures have made shipwreck of their lives.

Sublime Deliverance

It was in that late hour that Paul stood up to deliver his message of hope. There was a way out of their danger. If the vessel were surrendered to God; if the commands of the Great Captain were obeyed, all personnel aboard would succeed in reaching land. And since God's commands were given through His servant, Paul would have the final say concerning the navigation of the vessel. "And as the shipmen were about to flee out of the ship . . . Paul said, Except these abide in the ship, ye cannot be saved. Then the soldiers cut off the ropes of the boat, and let her fall off " (vv. 30-32). Wise men! They escaped death by inches. So it is in the greatest crises in life. There are storms from which only God can save.

THE RESURRECTION OF JESUS . . . the
message that changed the world

(1 CORINTHIANS 15)

The preaching of the resurrection of the Lord Jesus was easily the greatest bombshell ever to explode in the ancient world. So completely unexpected and catastrophic to Jewish policy, it was destined to have far-reaching repercussions. Immediately the Jewish world was divided into two sections, and the division has continued to this day. The leaders of the nation declared that the body of Jesus had been stolen; the apostles maintained that Christ had risen again from the dead, and that they had seen Him. If in the final analysis death overcame Jesus, then His ministry ended in defeat. We are therefore obliged to face the issue—either Christ rose again, or He remained in His tomb. In true Pauline fashion, let us consider a few propositions.

If Christ be Risen—Death is not the End

Perhaps the greatest enemy of mankind is death, for all human endeavour seems destined to terminate in a grave. The leading thinkers, the most brilliant of mortals, and all the sons of men walk along pathways which inevitably lead to a tomb. And ever since this ugly spectre came to darken man's outlook, he has asked the question, "If a man die, shall he live again?" (Job 14:14). Even prior to the proclamation of the Gospel message, the Jewish nation was divided on the subject. The Pharisees believed in the survival of the soul; the Sadducees declared that death terminated existence. Death is the fog barrier clouding distant horizons, and all people speculate as to what lies beyond the reach of mortal vision. If Christ rose again, then our greatest question is answered. Death cannot be the end.

If Christ be Risen—He is the World's Greatest Teacher

This is so because He accurately foretold the event. Constantly He warned His disciples that He would be delivered into the hands of sinful men, would be crucified, and after three days would rise again. That they forgot His message does not alter the fact that He predicted what was to take place. A striking comparison is provided in the case of one of Britain's leading spiritists, who declared that in proof of his faith, he would return after death to attend a special meeting to be convened in London. The meeting was held, and a great audience thronged the auditorium; yet to the disappointment of all, the famous prophet failed to appear. If Christ rose again in fulfilment of His promise, He alone of all the world's teachers was able to accomplish such a miracle.

If Christ be Risen—That is the Secret of New Testament Dynamic

Almost as great as the resurrection itself was the complete transformation in the disciples. Men who had fled from Gethsemane in order to save their lives, suddenly acquired a new power which enabled them to scorn the threat of death. Many of these early Christians were thrown to hungry lions; others were burnt at the stake, and "they held not their lives dear unto them." They challenged the power of heathen dynasties, and in their own life blood established the creed of their new faith. The resuscitation of their waning hopes, and the subsequent evangelizing of the world, demand that some explanation be given for this outstanding miracle. If Christ be risen, the problem is immediately solved.

If Christ be Risen—He is Still Accessible to Sinners

If Christ rose again to hide Himself in eternal remoteness, His action was entirely foreign to all that He previously taught, and completely lacking in wisdom. The Saviour never desired the life of a hermit, and constantly sought the presence of those who needed His help. If that same Saviour be risen again from the dead, it is certain that He can still be found by all who seek Him. If this were not true, the Gospel story would have an anti-climax that would make it the laughing-stock of the world. Critics would undoubtedly pinpoint the initial word of these propositions. They would ask how a seeker could be sure of the fact. The answer is very simple. Christ said, " Come unto me, all ye that labour and are heavy laden, and I will give you rest." Millions of men and women have accepted His invitation; and on the simple evidence that a dead Christ could do nothing, inward peace eloquently testifies to the reality of a risen Lord.

THE TWO WITNESSES . . . who fulfilled God's law

(2 CORINTHIANS 13:1)

According to Mosaic law, at least two witnesses were required in the conviction of a criminal. "Whoso killeth any person, the murderer shall be put to death by the mouth of witnesses: but one witness shall not testify against any person to cause him to die" (Num. 35:30). "One witness shall not rise up against a man for any iniquity, or for any sin, in any sin that he sinneth: at the mouth of two witnesses, or at the mouth of three witnesses, shall a matter be established" (Deut. 19:15). It is most interesting to note that in His relationships with the Lord Jesus Christ, God honoured His own laws.

The Two Witnesses of His Royalty (Matt. 3:16, 17)

"And Jesus, when he was baptized, went up straightway out of the water: and, lo, the heavens were opened unto him, and he saw the Spirit of God descending like a dove, and lighting upon him: and lo a voice from heaven, saying, This is my beloved Son, in whom I am well pleased." At the commencement of the public ministry of the Saviour, the remaining two members of the divine Family witnessed concerning the third (see chapter 42, "The Voice," p. 83). The redemption of the human race was the greatest undertaking ever handled by God. Other important missions had been entrusted to angels and prophets, but none of these were equal to the new task. God alone could redeem mankind, and since the law of the kinsman-redeemer insisted that the redeemer belonged to the same family as the slave, it became necessary for the Son of God to enter into our race. The story of Bethlehem reveals how this was accomplished.

The Two Witnesses of His Redemptive Work (Luke 9:28-31)

"And as Jesus prayed, the fashion of his countenance was altered . . . And behold there talked with him two men, which were Moses and Elias: who appeared in glory, and spake of his decease which he should accomplish at Jerusalem." God's choice of witnesses was most admirable. These two saints of a bygone age represented both the law and the prophets. Moses, whose very name suggested the written word, and Elijah, the foremost of the prophets, appeared to add their testimony concerning the value of the Son of God. While the synagogue leaders openly proclaimed their allegiance to the ancient patriarchs, Moses and Elijah appeared to speak with Christ concerning the crucifixion. Thus they confessed that Jesus would fulfil all they had believed and promised.

The Two Witnesses of His Resurrection (John 20:11-12)

" But Mary stood without at the sepulchre weeping: and as she wept, she stooped down, and looked into the sepulchre, and seeth two angels in white sitting, the one at the head, and the other at the feet, where the body of Jesus had lain. And they say unto her, Woman, why weepest thou? " The memory of that wonderful morning never left Mary. She heard from the angels the glad tidings of the resurrection, and a little while later she recognized her Lord. The two angels came to speak of the resurrection, for they had witnessed the thrilling event and were able to comfort the sorrowful woman. Neither the untruths of the Jewish story nor the false statements of modern teaching can change the testimony of the two angels who witnessed His triumph.

The Two Witnesses of His Return (Acts 1:9-11)

" While they beheld, Jesus was taken up; and a cloud received him out of their sight. And while they looked stedfastly toward heaven as he went up, behold, two men stood by them in white apparel; which also said, Ye men of Galilee, why stand ye gazing up into heaven? this same Jesus, which is taken up from you into heaven, shall so come in like manner as ye have seen him go into heaven." The return of the Lord Jesus is the greatest hope of the Church, and there are many students who believe the fulfilment of this great promise cannot long be delayed. In the mouth of the two witnesses the testimony has been established. The Gospel story is the most reasonable message in the world, for at each crucial point in the ministry of Jesus, God honoured His laws and through the united testimony of reliable witnesses, endorsed the teaching of the Saviour. " Even so, come, Lord Jesus " (Rev. 22:20).

PAUL . . . and God's answer to a sceptical world

There is an interesting contrast in the Gospel story. We are told that the people looked at the dying Saviour and exclaimed, "Let him now come down from the cross, and we will believe him" (Matt. 27:42). Yet that order was reversed when Christ spoke to Martha in Bethany. He said, "If thou wouldest believe, thou shouldest see the glory of God" (John 11:40). In the economy of God, faith foreruns vision, for it is "the substance of things hoped for, the evidence of things not seen" (Heb. 11:1). The infidel declares that no tangible evidence can be found to prove the reality of God; yet the humblest Christian constantly discovers the facts the existence of which is denied by the people whose hearts are barren of faith.

The Lord Jesus Christ is Able to Save (Heb. 7:25)

"Wherefore he is able also to save them to the uttermost that come unto God by him, seeing he ever liveth to make intercession for them." The Christians of the early Church were soon called upon to face great persecution. Some of the best Roman governors were the most fierce enemies, for believing that the denial of their pagan gods would bring disaster upon the empire, they used all means at their disposal to annihilate the new movement. Christians were fed to hungry lions, and even burnt at the stake. Such opposition shook the faith of the people, and many were tempted to return to their former beliefs. Yet the Jewish converts still encountered difficulty, for the temple life had ceased, and the daily offering was no longer placed upon the altar. Caught between the cessation of the old system of worship and the unparalleled persecution of the new, the weaklings of the Church faltered and questioned their leaders. The writer of the epistle to the Hebrews explained that the living Christ superseded all acts of priesthood, and now lived at God's right hand to make intercession for His people. *And the greatest evidence in favour of this fact was His ability to save.* Every miracle constituted a challenge to agnosticism, and every transformed life an indication of Christ's power.

The Lord Jesus Christ is Able to Keep (2 Tim. 1:12)

"... for I know whom I have believed, and am persuaded that he is able to keep that which I have committed unto him against that day." This represents one of the most triumphant declarations of Pauline doctrines. When Timothy visited his great leader to sit with him in the prison cell, many questions filled the mind of the younger man. There at his side was the indomitable Paul, who could say, " Of the Jews five times received I forty stripes save one. Thrice was I beaten with rods, once was I stoned, thrice I suffered shipwreck, a night and a day I have been in the deep " (2 Cor. 11:24-25). Other people had long since slipped back into error; yet this brave apostle had persistently continued along his appointed course. Nothing had been permitted to prevent his following Christ, and now at the end of his journey he was able to say, " Henceforth there is laid up for me a crown of righteousness " (2 Tim. 4:8). The secret of Paul's continuance lay in the keeping power of his Lord. He said, " Not I, but Christ liveth in me "; " He is able to keep," and his life-story endorsed the truth of his testimony.

The Lord Jesus Christ is Able to do the Impossible (Eph. 3:20)

" Now unto him that is able to do exceeding abundantly above all that we ask or think, according to the power that worketh in us." This is a superlative verse, and is all the more remarkable because it was addressed to the Church at Ephesus. The assembly in that leading city of Asia had been born in much travail. The heathen worshippers of Diana had striven to overthrow the Church, and even Paul had been in danger of losing his life. In an amazing fashion the power of God had triumphed over all opposition, and under the leadership of their beloved minister the Church had continued to grow and had witnessed many miracles. Then Paul declared, " He is able to do still far greater things. He can do more than the wildest imaginations would consider possible—exceeding abundantly above all you can ask or think." There were times when Paul revealed a daring disregard for the constraining laws of grammar. He mixed his superlatives in the most bewildering fashion, for language seemed utterly inadequate to express the wonder of his message.

THE APOSTLE PETER . . . who graduated in
God's university

Simon Peter has always been one of the most attractive of the apostolic figures. In many senses he might be described as the Elijah of the New Testament, for one cannot read his story without feeling here is a man of like passions as we are. The big fisherman, as he has been called, alternately knew the depths of despair and the heights of joy. He seemed to be intensely human, and in spite of obvious deficiencies was used of God to strike the earliest blow against the powers of darkness. Perhaps the only school he attended was God's school; but a study of the second epistle of Peter will clearly reveal how he mastered his lessons and graduated from the classroom.

Standard One in the Knowledge of God

This is clearly set forth for us in 2 Peter 2:20, "... they have escaped the pollutions of the world through *the knowledge of the Lord and Saviour Jesus Christ . . .*" This is the first lesson taught in God's seminary. When a man enrols as a student, he does so as a sinner. His coming to God admits of two things. First, the would-be student confesses that he has need to learn. Secondly, he expresses his faith that this, and only this, is the school where his needs can be met. Thus he escapes " the pollutions of the world." Many would call this experience " conversion," but whatever name might be given for the event, it is unquestionably the beginning of all the training given by the divine Master.

Standard Two in the Knowledge of God

" Grace and peace be multiplied unto you *through the knowledge of God, and of Jesus our Lord*" (2 Peter 1:2). Peace comes through faith in the Lord Jesus. It is the inevitable result of our justification by faith (Rom. 5:1). *Multiplied peace* is a definite advance on peace, for the blessings experienced through salvation are increased a thousandfold as we advance in God's school. There we learn of the " exceeding great and precious promises "— the guarantee that in all the vicissitudes of life, God will be sufficient.

Standard Three in the Knowledge of God

" According as his divine power hath given unto us all things that pertain unto life and godliness, *through the knowledge of him* that hath called us to glory and virtue " (2 Peter 1:3). The Christian student is now really beginning to make headway with his studies. Conversion leads first to consecration, and then to sanctification. Grace not only means salvation *from the uttermost;* it also introduces the convert to a greater aspect of the work of God. Man is saved *to the uttermost.* " All things that pertain unto life and godliness " are part of the equipment of the saint. Multiplied grace imparts the power which enables one to triumph over the power of inbred sin. The old man, with all the affections and lusts thereof, is crucified, and in place of the old interests comes a new life which is called godliness.

Standard Four in the Knowledge of God

" For if these things be in you, and abound, they make you that ye shall neither be barren nor unfruitful in *the knowledge of our Lord Jesus Christ* " (2 Peter 1:8). During His great discourse about the Vine, the Lord Jesus said, " If ye abide in me, and my words abide in you, ye shall ask what ye will, and it shall be done unto you. Herein is my Father glorified, that ye bear much fruit . . ." (John 15:7, 8). And, " the fruit of the Spirit is love, joy, peace, long-suffering, gentleness, goodness, faith, meekness, temperance: against such there is no law " (Gal. 5:22-23). It is a natural sequence that the fruit of a godly life will be followed by fruitful service.

Standard Five in the Knowledge of God

" But grow in grace, *and in the knowledge of our Lord and Saviour Jesus Christ* " (2 Pet. 3:18). And so at the end of his great epistle Peter, as with the wave of a hand, indicates the limitless expanse of God's great world where, in practical experience, our spiritual education may be developed and advanced. The university of heaven is the greatest centre of learning in the world. There are no entrance exams., and no would-be scholar is ever turned away. The only condition for enrolment is that scholars should present their applications for admittance at Calvary.

JAMES . . . who disliked one-sided Christians
(JAMES 1-5)

The apostle James declares that true faith always begets good works. A faith without expression is a tree without branches. Preaching unsupported by virtuous conduct is a noise without meaning. Again and again he stresses this important point, and even suggests that in spite of man's profession, his salvation is in question if his professed faith in Christ does not lead to daily righteousness. In the light of this theme, it is truly remarkable to discover that James has much to say about prayer. This is one of the "good works," and is a practical expression of faith.

The Confident Prayer

"If any of you lack wisdom, let him ask of God, that giveth to all men liberally, and upbraideth not; and it shall be given him. *But let him ask in faith, nothing wavering*" (James 1:5, 6). It is quite useless to proclaim the wonder of prayer if we fail to practise what we preach. The Lord has given His promise that if we ask anything according to His will, "*it shall be done.*" Radiant confidence banishes doubt, and is as much a good work as the helping hand stretched forth to assist a fellow man. Alas, so many saints are like Rhoda of old, who having prayed for the release of Simon Peter, found it difficult to believe that God answered her prayer, and that Peter was standing outside the door waiting to be admitted.

The Constant Prayer

". . . ye have not, because ye ask not " (James 4:2). James probably remembered the words of the Saviour, " Men ought always to pray, and not to faint " (Luke 18:1). It is not always essential to go aside to a secret place to commune with the Father. The Lord Jesus often went to Olivet, but His daily attitude was one of ceaseless dependence upon God. We should never neglect the specified place of prayer, but if a man's heart be attuned to the Highest, he may pray even as he walks down the street.

> Prayer is the burden of a sigh,
> The falling of a tear;
> The upward glancing of an eye
> When none but God is near.

The Conscientious Prayer

" Ye ask, and receive not, because ye ask amiss . . ."
(James 4:3). The true Christian is one who sincerely
seeks the will of God in all matters. Simon the sorcerer
sought the power of the Holy Spirit—not because he would
glorify God, but rather that he himself might become
famous (Acts 8:18, 19). Hannah often prayed for a son, in
order to satisfy the innate yearnings of her own heart. Yet
when she prayed, " Give unto thine handmaid a man child,
and I will give him unto the Lord all the days of his life,"
the Lord graciously answered her petition (1 Sam. 1:11,
19). Selfish prayers may be expressed in superb phraseology; may attract the praise of men, and yet be a waste
of time. If I ask in order to satisfy my own pride, I am
lacking in good works, for the Christian's chief end is to
glorify his Lord.

The Collective Prayer

" Is any sick among you? Let him call for the elders of
the church; and let them pray over him, anointing him with
oil in the name of the Lord: and the prayer of faith shall
save the sick, and the Lord shall raise him up; and if he
have committed sins, they shall be forgiven him " (James
5:14, 15). To a very large extent the miraculous healing
of the sick is a lost art of the Church, and where it is
practised, often undignified conduct on the part of the
practitioners brings discredit upon the Lord whose name
they use. It can never be emphasized too much that God
can and *does* heal the sick, but it is wrong to assume that
healing is always in the will of God. There are occasions
when He deliberately places His child aside in order to
teach in sickness the lessons unknown in health. Some of
the world's choicest saints have been among the greatest
sufferers. Yet this cannot excuse the prayerless, powerless
Church. If we believe in the unchanging Christ, we believe
that He can still perform His miracles just as He did long
ago. Let us, then, pray in faith, for the world respects a
living Church.

> O Thou, by whom we come to God,
> The Life, the Truth, the Way;
> The path of prayer Thyself hast trod,
> Lord, teach us how to pray.

THE WEALTHY CHURCH . . . that went bankrupt

(REVELATION 3:14, 22)

When a wealthy man becomes insolvent there is something radically wrong either in his soul or in his business. If his material possessions cannot prevent disaster, moral weakness in his life has created problems too great to be solved by money. If his business be based on unsound principles, virtue and sincerity will be unequal to the task of satisfying creditors. The Church of the Laodiceans provides a striking example of a bankrupt assembly. They had a great bank balance, but an empty prayer room. They had many social connections, but no sincere converts. They found it easy to obtain phenomenal collections, but tears were unknown. It was a popular social club with a religious flavour about its proceedings, and never a birthplace for souls. And it was to this Church that the Lord Jesus sent His challenging message: " Behold, I stand at the door, and knock . . ."

It is possible to be very religious and not be a Christian

This simple fact explains why Christ said, " Behold, I stand at the door, and knock." We must never forget this letter was sent to a *Church*. The Lord declared, " Thou sayest, I am rich, and increased with goods, and have need of nothing; and knowest not that thou art wretched, and miserable, and poor, and blind, and naked." This was the Church that possessed everything and enjoyed nothing. Their acts of worship were formalities; their sermons were essays meant to please; their prayers were beautifully phrased utterances that charmed the listeners but never reached the heart of God. They had a form of godliness, but no living Christ who breathed peace into troubled hearts.

It is not possible to be lukewarm and not to be in danger

It is worthy of note that these people were not " cold." Had they been completely cold, the message delivered to them might have been somewhat different. They were neither hot nor cold. They occupied a position about halfway between the two extremes. They were sufficiently warm to go to church; and sufficiently cold to keep Christ outside the door. To these people Jesus said, " I will spue thee out of my mouth." The most difficult people to reach with the Gospel are the men and women who respectably occupy the middle position. To the arrogant sinner they say, " You should be a better man "; to the Christian they say, " You are too narrow-minded." They have sufficient vision to recognise their own importance, but are too blind to see their own nakedness. Such people inevitably stand in great danger.

It is not possible for Christ to enter a man's life without the man's permission

The human heart is a temple, of which man is the custodian. It is a strange thing that the Maker of heaven and earth can be easily frustrated by the closed door of a human sanctuary. This explains why the Lord Jesus found it necessary to ask admittance to the inmost shrine of the Laodicean Church. It explains also why the same state of affairs exists throughout the world. Christ respects the free will of man. He may so easily control the storm on Galilee's lake; He may instantly expel demons from their place of abode; He might seem capable of performing the impossible: yet when He comes to the human threshold, He can only knock and ask the tenant to draw back the bolts.

It is not possible to have Christ within and be bankrupt

Language is inadequate to express the wonder of His promise, " I will come in to him, and will sup with him, and he with me." The Saviour always left a place richer than when He entered. His message to this disappointing church spoke of " gold tried in the fire . . . white raiment that thou mayest be clothed . . . eyesalve that thou mayest see." No man can be poor when Christ dwells within his heart. All the promises of God are " yea and amen " in the Lord Jesus; and if He be my constant companion, I have access to the unlimited wealth of eternal banks. It is a cause for great amazement that such a wealthy Saviour should seek a home in a sinner's heart. It is even more surprising that some hearts are locked against Him. The poor Laodiceans went bankrupt, and they had no excuse.

THE PRETTIEST SIGHT IN HEAVEN

(REVELATION 4:3)

" And, behold, a throne was set in heaven . . . *and there was a rainbow round about the throne, in sight like unto an emerald."* The rainbow and the throne are two opposites, and yet they belong to each other. The former was placed in the clouds after the great deluge, to be the sign of God's covenant with man never to repeat the catastrophe. The rainbow speaks of mercy. The throne is the symbol or seat of divine authority, where God rules in equity. When John was permitted to look into heaven, he marvelled for the rainbow around the throne expressed the greatest truth in holy Scripture.

The Mercy of God Always Overshadows His Judgments

The Old Testament writers recorded four outstanding acts of judgment, and in each of these the rainbow was about the throne. (i) The great deluge of Noah's time was prefaced by a long period of earnest preaching, when Noah warned his fellow men of impending disaster. And even after Noah and his family had entered the ark, the Lord still waited seven days before the rains were allowed to fall. (ii) The midnight judgment on Egypt was prefaced by the warnings of God given to Pharaoh, and even on the night of doom a way of escape was provided for all who had accepted the offer of sheltering behind the blood of the lamb which had been sprinkled on the doorposts. (iii) The destruction of the Canaanites as illustrated by the fall of Jericho revealed that even for the greatest sinner a way of escape had been provided. Rahab the harlot placed a scarlet thread in her window, and all within that house were saved. (iv) The fall of Jerusalem and the subsequent captivity in Babylon revealed that God had sent His prophets to warn Israel, and even when the people rejected His admonitions He still preserved a remnant in the land of bondage. God's judgments may seem severe, but keen eyes will always detect the rainbow around the throne.

The Mercy of God is Something of Exquisite Beauty

" In sight like unto an emerald." As the light of the glory of God played on the sombre clouds of justice, the sign of the mercy of God shone forth in scintillating beauty. It was a jewel of the skies. The mercy of God is the most wonderful thing in the world. (i) *It is undisguised.* A rainbow cannot be hidden, unless one can extinguish the sun. Even so no man can hide the mercy of God, unless he be able to remove the Lord Jesus. Mercy is evident in all God's dealings with man. (ii) *It is undeserved.* Each one of the Old Testament examples provides an illustration of this truth. The first mention of a rainbow is found in Genesis 9:13, where the bow is seen in the clouds. The next reference is found in Ezekiel 1:28, where the sign of God's mercy is found amid the evil evidences of Babylonian idolatry. (iii) *It is unequalled.* There has never been a substitute for a rainbow, nor for the mercy of God. They stand alone in splendid isolation, and are exclusively connected with God and the sun.

The Mercy of God is Still Extended to Man

The fourth and final reference to a rainbow is perhaps the greatest of all. " And I saw another mighty angel come down from heaven, clothed with a cloud: and a rainbow was upon His head. . . . And He had in His hand a little book open. . . . And He said to me, Take the little book and eat it up; and it shall make thy inmost being bitter, but it shall be in thy mouth sweet as honey. And I took the little book and ate it up. . . . And he said unto me, Thou must prophecy again before many peoples and nations and tongues and kings " (Rev. 10:1, 10). The last book of the Bible has many things to say concerning the everlasting kingdom, when the tabernacle of God shall be with men. The coming of that glorious day will bring either supreme happiness or eternal sorrow to mankind. It is truly significant that prior to that era the angel with the rainbow is sent to commission a preacher to make known the message of the " little book." God is still desirous to welcome additional guests to the marriage supper of the Lamb, and every preacher who has first " eaten " the little book will cry aloud to the nations, " Today if ye will hear His voice, harden not your hearts."

THE EVANGELIST AND HIS TASK

Whenever a young man tells me that he would like to become an evangelist, my reactions always confound him. I strongly urge that if he can possibly avoid the calling, to do so. No one should ever contemplate the full-time ministry in the Kingdom of God, unless the urge is inescapable. If the call becomes unbearable; if it becomes a case of responding to God's call or losing interest in life, then the candidate will have some chance of succeeding amid the difficulties of the field of service. Therefore my advice always runs true to type. Avoid by every possible means the way that leads to full-time service for God. If the call cannot be avoided, a man may be sure that God has chosen him.

A thrilling evangelistic meeting can be exceedingly inspiring, and every student may become unbalanced in his judgments just because glorious enthusiasm has thrilled his soul. After one such meeting, a man said to the Lord Jesus, "Lord, I will follow thee whithersoever thou goest." His fiery zeal was overshadowed by the Master's answer: "Foxes have holes, and birds of the air have nests; but the Son of man hath not where to lay his head." There is no further record of the man's activity, and it would seem that he returned to his home. To imagine that an evangelistic career brings unclouded skies and unending experiences of joyful activities, is a great mistake. Yet, if the Lord leads one into such realms of service, the compensations outnumber any sacrifices which might be demanded. The world needs Spirit-filled evangelists; special men, specially equipped to do a special task. Whenever revival has enriched the Church, this unique ministry has been well to the fore. Sometimes the graduate of the university has been in the place of eminence; sometimes the ordained cleric has been brought to the forefront; but within the last fifty years, the Principality of Wales had evidence that an ordinary young fellow could be used by God to do the impossible.

It is true that the young pastor Timothy was told to do the work of an evangelist, but that did not alter the fact that the New Testament Church encouraged itinerant evangelists. There are those who say that according to Pauline doctrines the task of evangelising was entrusted to the local minister; but every student of the Bible will know that in reality the teaching of Paul is opposed to the modern idea. Without the pioneer missionary, the cause of Christ might have stayed in Jerusalem and its environs. The evangelist was a man who went into the unknown, to seek souls for Christ. It would appear that Paul urged Timothy to do the work of an evangelist because he realized that unless some of the same holy fire filled the pastor's heart, the Church under his care would never play its part in extending the Kingdom of God. To suggest that the itinerant, pioneer evangelist is no longer needed, borders on the ludicrous. One might be justified in suggesting that he was never more needed than he is today. The customs and the peoples of the world may be changing, and undoubtedly God's servant will need to be aware of the varying circumstances of his far-flung parish. He will need to be very versatile; but there can never be any doubt that God gave evangelists to the Church because He deemed it was necessary so to do. These men were easily recognized. They were brought into the work, sometimes against their will, and yet as they went forth in the name of Christ, divine strength was made perfect in their weakness. The Church of the present day urgently needs men of this calibre, for no one could deny that in many parts of the so-called Christian world, the majority of the population never enter a church, and have no respect for those who do. It would seem that the days are gone when the voice of the pulpit counted in the decisions of the nations.

The churches of all denominations have recognized these evil tendencies, and many of the world's greatest thinkers declare that unless supernatural forces can again be introduced into human affairs, anarchy will become irresistible. Theological circles agree, but seem unable to produce a remedy. We have many ministers and some travelling evangelists, but our greatest need is for a race of prophets —men who fear God and fear nobody else. If such men can be found quickly, our world will be saved from disaster.

Yet the greatest opponents of this view would probably be found within the Church itself. It is an indisputable fact that at the present time evangelism has been brought into disrepute, and many clergymen refuse to participate in special campaigning. A great amount of criticism has been spoken against the itinerant preacher, and perhaps some of this has been fully deserved. Certain things have been done in the name of evangelism that make many Christians shudder. Nevertheless, we must see things in a true perspective. It is a staggering thought that many of the ministers who decry the evangelist themselves preach to dying Churches. When the local Church is two-thirds empty; when the prayer meetings are non-existent; when the saints are yearning for a breath of heaven; and when souls are very seldom if ever won for Christ in his meetings, the minister of that Church should be the last man to criticize another. Every true evangelist welcomes criticism from a man whom God is honouring; a man whose Church radiates divine life to the community; a man whose efforts are continually pointing souls to Christ. Yet when the custodian of a religious refrigerator tries to tell an evangelist how to win souls, and at the same time has never reached one himself, his actions betray a shallowness of spirituality, an overwhelming sense of egoism, and to say the least, the presence of a super-abundance of arrogant cheek. It is a sad fact that the people who know best how to bring revival to the Churches, generally preach to empty pews.

On the other hand, thank God, there are many, many fine men in our Churches, and the evangelist should be careful to help these servants of God at every opportunity. All campaign meetings should be noteworthy for the absence of appeals for money. The man who constantly advertises his poverty succeeds in revealing his pitiable lack of faith. The old slogan, " Pray and tell God's people," may be workable in some instances, but it should always be obnoxious in evangelistic crusades. I shall always be thankful for the example set before the Pilgrim Preachers—the itinerant band to which I once belonged. Old Mr. Ernest Luff often lectured his " boys " on the subject of prayer and personal needs. He asked us never to pray for money if strangers were present in our prayer meetings. He insisted that, if we did so, we were not speaking to the Lord but to the man kneeling next to us. If local friends were absent, we could pray as often and as long as we desired. We had neither committee nor collections, but our needs were always fully met. Indeed, had we depended upon appeals to people, we should have lost the greatest of all our experiences. If prayer is answered, then let every evangelist depend upon the Lord for finance, and not constantly beg from all and sundry. An evangelistic beggar is not a good advertisement of God's faithfulness.

Another difficulty arises from the fact that many people declare that the converts of evangelistic missions disappear too quickly. The special meetings are said to be an unsettling tidal wave, which leaves behind a nasty and dirty backwash. Many ministers fear this, and on the assumption that prevention is better than cure, they refuse to permit evangelistic meetings in their Churches. This is a great problem, but there are two ways of looking at it. First, every minister should be aware of the fact that post-campaign days will bring to his own heart a great challenge. The evangelist is a doctor brought in to assist with the birth of the spiritual child. The Church and the minister must be the mother of the child during its entire life-time. If the mother starves her baby to death, it will be criminal to charge the doctor with incompetency. No minister must take things for granted, for each new day will present a new challenge. The man who is too old to learn has outlived his usefulness. But having said that, we need to consider another issue. There may be many people who will disagree with my statement, but I firmly believe that every evangelist should deal with his own converts. I would never entrust the control of my enquiry room to a band of workers. There are many fine Christians who excel in personal work, but sometimes the most enthusiastic of the workers are the least capable of handling seeking souls. When I decided for the Lord Jesus, the minister of the local Church asked three questions. What is your name? How old are you? Have you ever done this before? Then with a final " God bless you," he walked away. I was only a youth, but it took nine months of patient searching the Scriptures to discover what he might have told me that night. I vowed then that if ever I had the opportunity of leading a soul to Christ, I would endeavour to do the job well. Thus I have made it my practice to take charge personally of my enquiry room; and I commend this to others.

Concerning methods of conducting a mission, I have little to say. Every man must be himself, for if ever he succumbs to the temptation of aping another, the death-knell will have sounded on his career. God made me to be myself; I must not disappoint my Creator. I am constantly asked about the advisability of using films, organizing quiz programmes, and other unusual items to attract people into the services. There, again, the young evangelist must be careful. In this modern age, films draw great crowds; yet some of the older Christians would be shocked —as they express it—if their Church became a picture house. Every man doing this special work will need to look constantly to Christ for guidance in these matters. I think I would use or do anything which would bring souls to the Saviour. Perhaps I am fortunate, for I have never had to resort to anything but the straightforward preaching of the grand old Gospel. I belong to Wales, where the sermon still occupies the vital place in the meeting. As a son of that favoured land, I have followed in the footsteps of my forebears; and I trust I shall never deem it necessary to change my style. I still believe that the old Bible scenes, attractively presented, will fascinate and grip the people of any age. My meetings invariably end in 80 minutes, and more often than not, 45-50 minutes of that time are devoted to the presentation of the message. There is no need to elaborate on the doctrines preached, for they are found in every Bible sketch included in this and my other books.

Finally, I would mention another important matter. It is my opinion that unless the Church members become soul seekers, the task of the evangelist will be impossible. It is a cause for regret that in these days of high pressure organization, many Christians have degenerated into sermon tasters. The evangelistic meeting has become a spiritual picnic ground, where the relative values of various speakers are compared and contrasted. I have often seen hundreds of people patiently queueing to gain admittance to my service, and I have sighed, wishing they had spent the time inviting passers-by to the meeting. Over and over again, when I have whispered to a fellow minister, " How many unconverted people are present tonight?" I have heard his answer, " I don't really know, but I think we have a few." The entire purpose of the evangelistic crusade will be frustrated unless we can attract into the meetings those who so urgently need Christ. I am quite sure that there will never be an effective substitute for the warm-hearted interest displayed in the affectionate invitation given by one man to his friend. If the work of seeking outsiders be left to the

INDEX

Combined and Comprehensive Bible Index Covering Bible Cameos—Bible Pinnacles—Bible Treasures

GENESIS:						PAGE
1:26	...	B. Treasures	...	...	...	114
2:8-9	...	B. Pinnacles	...	...	...	19
2:21-22	...	B. Pinnacles	...	...	...	1
3:10	...	B. Cameos	...	...	...	1
3:22	...	B. Cameos	...	...	...	131
3:22-24	...	B. Pinnacles	...	...	...	19
3:24	...	B. Pinnacles	...	...	...	6
4:1-10	...	B. Pinnacles	...	...	...	3
4:16-26	...	B. Treasures	...	...	...	1
5:21-22	...	B. Treasures	...	...	...	3
5:24	...	B. Pinnacles	...	...	...	5
6:20	...	B. Cameos	...	...	...	3
7:10	...	B. Pinnacles	...	...	...	167
9:4	...	B. Treasures	...	...	...	145
9:13	...	B. Pinnacles	...	...	...	168
13:1-4	...	B. Cameos	...	...	...	5
13:7-18	...	B. Treasures	...	...	...	5
18:9-15	...	B. Pinnacles	...	...	...	7
18:27	...	B. Treasures	...	...	...	7
19:16-22	...	B. Cameos	...	...	...	7
19:17	...	B. Treasures	...	...	...	9
19:26	...	B. Treasures	...	...	...	9
21:5	...	B. Pinnacles	...	...	...	9
21:14-19	...	B. Cameos	...	...	...	130
22:5	...	B. Pinnacles	...	...	...	9
22:8	...	B. Pinnacles	...	...	...	10
22:15-18	...	B. Pinnacles	...	...	...	10
24:1-10	...	B. Pinnacles	...	...	...	11
24:58-67	...	B. Pinnacles	...	...	...	11
25:21	...	B. Pinnacles	...	...	...	12
25:29-34	...	B. Cameos	...	...	...	11
26:18	...	B. Cameos	...	...	...	9
27:38	...	B. Cameos	...	...	...	12
28:2-11	...	B. Pinnacles	...	...	...	13
28:10-17	...	B. Pinnacles	...	...	...	13
32:24-35	...	B. Cameos	...	...	...	13
37:41	...	B. Cameos	...	...	...	15
50:25	...	B. Treasures	...	...	...	11
EXODUS:						
3:4	...	B. Treasures	...	...	...	13
3:13-14	...	B. Treasures	...	...	...	122